# The Armenian Troubles and the Ottoman Empire: The Views of a Nineteenth Century American Convert to Islam

Muhammad Alexander Russell Webb
Magribine Press

Magribine Press
5333 W. Rosedale Ave.
Chicago, IL 60646-6539
Send all Correspondence Attn: Muhammed al-Ahari

Cataloguing information for the original texts:

Title: *A Few Facts about Turkey under the Reign of Abdul Hamid II*
Publisher: New York: Press of J.J. Little & Co., 1895.
Description: 67 p.; 23 cm.
Subjects: Abdülhamid II, Sultan of the Turks, 1842-1918.
        Turkey – History – 1878-1909.
Call number: F297 F43

Title: *The Armenian Troubles and Where the Responsibility Lies*
Publisher: New York: Press of J.J. Little & Co., 1895.
Subjects: Armenian massacres, 1894-1896 – Turkey – Sason – Foreign
        public opinion, American – History – Sources.
        Armenians – Turkey – Sason – History – 19th century.
        Sason (Turkey) – Ethnic relations – History.
Notes: "The five letters now published in this pamphlet were originally
        reproduced by an influential newspaper of New York. They
        were written and sent from Constantinople."
Call number: F604 AR
Description: 35 p. 23 cm.

# Table of Contents

# Muhammad Alexander Russell Webb, Islam in America, & the American Islamic Propagation Movement
by
## Muhammed A. Al-Ahari

Muhammad Alexander Russell Webb was born on November 9, 1846 in Hudson, New York to Mr. and Mrs. Alexander Nelson Webb. A.N. Webb was a leading journalist of his day and perhaps influenced his son's later journalistic exploits. The young Webb received his early education at the Home School in Glendale, Massachusetts and later attended college at Claverack College near Hudson, New York. As a youth he worked in some of the finer jewelry houses of New York, but quickly turned to journalism. He excelled in college and upon finishing school purchased a weekly newspaper in Unionville, Missouri and became the publisher. The prowess as a journalist was soon apparent and he was offered city editorship of the St. Joseph, Missouri Daily Gazette. Next he became associate editor of the Missouri Morning Journal. Later he became one of the editors at the Missouri Republican in St. Louis. This newspaper was the second oldest and largest daily newspaper at that time. Over the years, he eventually edited or worked for seven newspapers in Missouri, New Jersey, and New York.

While working for the Missouri Republican, he was appointed (in September 1887) by President Cleveland to be Consular Representative to the Philippines at the U.S. office at Manila.

According to the editor of his book *The Three Lectures*, he had given up any concept of religion at least fifteen years before that point. He started his life as a Presbyterian but found it dull and restraining. As early as 1881 he started a search for his true faith by reading in books from a well stocked library of over 13,000 volumes that he had access to. He started his study with Buddhism and finding it lacking, he began to study Islam. In 1888, he formally declared himself Muslim.

At that time he had yet to meet a Muslim but was put in contact with several Muslims in India by a local Parsi businessman. A newspaper publisher, Badruddin Abdullah Kur of Bombay, published several of Webb's letters in his paper. A local businessman, Hajji Abdullah Arab, saw these letters and went to Manila to see Webb.

After the visit, Webb began plans to tour India and then return to the U.S. to propagate Islam. Webb's wife, Ella G. Webb, and their three children had also accepted Islam. Hajji Abdullah returned to India and raised funds for Webb's tour. Webb visited Poona, Bombay, Calcutta, Hyderabad, and Madras and gave speeches in each town. All are published at least once separately and some are published in collection.

He resigned his post in 1892 and toured India then returned to the U.S. His family stayed in San Francisco till he sent for them. Settling in New York, he established the Oriental Publishing Company at 1122 Upper Broadway. This company published his writings (including his magnum opus *Islam in America*). Islam in America contained 70 pages divided into eight chapters namely: I) Why I Became a Muslim; II) An Outline of Islamic Faith; III) The Five Pillars of Practice; IV) Islam in Its Philosophic Aspect; V) Polygamy and the Purdah; VI) Popular Errors Refuted; VII) The Muslim Defensive Wars; and, VIII) The American Islamic Propaganda. Along with this venture he started the organ of the American Muslim Propagation Movement called Muslim World. The first issue appeared May 12, 1893 and was dedicated to "The Interests of the American Islamic Propaganda" and "To spread the light of Islam in America". It lasted for seven monthly issues (May to November 1893).

Webb was the main representative for Islam at the 1893 World Parliament of Religions in Chicago. On September 20th and 21st, 1893, he gave two speeches. His speeches were entitled: "The Influence of Islam upon Social Conditions" and "The Spirit of Islam" and were published in the large two volume proceedings of the Parliament called "The First World's Parliament of Religions" (1894).

For the rest of his life he was the main spokesman for Islam in America. Many of America's most prominent thinkers heard him speak on the graces of the Islamic Faith. This included the author of Tom Sawyer – Mark Twain. On Broadway, in Manhattan, he founded a short lived mosque. The reasons for the termination of this Masjid are unknown, but it could be due to a lack of financial support from India. Throughout the rest of America he started study circles. Chicago, Washington, D.C., Newark, Manhattan, Kansas City, Philadelphia, Pittsburgh, and Cleveland were the sites of some of them. They were named Mecca Study Circle No. 1 (NYC), Qur'an Study Circle, Capital Study Circle No. 4, etc. each using an Islamic city or reference in the title. It is likely they studied Webb's works and those he suggested. The last meeting was in 1943 in Manhattan.

He is also known for his writing two booklets about the Armenian and Turkish Wars from a Muslim point of view[1] and for being appointed the Honorary Turkish Consul in New York by Sultan Abdul Hamid II. The Sultan had been shown plans by Webb for a Muslim cemetery and Masjid and complimented Webb on them. Unfortunately these plans never materialized.

Webb two works on Turkey were published anonymously, but were publicized by his newspapers and were reviewed by several newspapers and religious publications of his time. *The Open Court* gave a brief positive comment,

> "Persons desirous of studying the Armenian question from a Turkish standpoint will find the same ably represented by a pamphlet called The Armenian Troubles and Where the Responsibility Lies, by Muhammad Alexander Russell Webb, Ulster Park, Ulster County, New York. Mr. Webb is an American proselyte to Muhammadanism."[2]

Webb's work for Sultan Abdul Hamid won him honors from the Ottoman Empire, but it also resulted in editorials that either

---

[1] *The Armenian Troubles and Where the Responsibility Lies* and *A Few Facts about Turkey under the Rule of Abdul Hamid II* are reprinted herein.
[2] *The Open Court*, Vol. X-30, No. 465, July 23, 1896, p. 4998.

downplayed the importance of his work or called it lies and propaganda.

A more positive example can be found in the following article – "Turkish Railroads and Industries".[3]

"An interesting little book has just been issued, entitled, "A Few Facts about Turkey under the Reign of Abdul Hamid II." It is written by "An American Observer" (M. I. Alexander Russell Webb, Ulster Park, Ulster Co., N.Y.), and is intended to show the wonderful progress which has been made by Turkey under its present Sultan. The author thinks that the development and advancement which has been steadily going on ever since the present Turkish sovereign ascended the imperial throne deserves to be brought before the English-speaking people.

"Railroads Of Turkey.—A simple enumeration of the railroads constructed since His Majesty ascended the throne, or which are now in construction, as well as the concessions accorded to railroads, and which will from one moment to another be put into execution, will suffice to show how much the Ottoman empire owes to the Sultan Abdul Hamid. If today one can go from Paris to Constantinople by rail in less than four days, it is incontestably to the continued and persevering efforts of the Sultan Abdul Hamid that this great result is due. It is he who in the "Conference of Four" did not cease to insist upon the joining of the railroads of Roumelia to those of Central Europe, and the other countries must be grateful to him for the accomplishment of this great work.

"Manufactories Of Constantinople.—In the capital and its suburbs are large industrial establishments which can defy all comparison with those of the Occident, of which some, established formerly, have received from the incessant care and attention of the Sultan a second life, as it were. Such are the manufactory of the military cloths of Fezhané, the superb workshops of the "Grand Maîtrise" of Artillery at Tophane and the dockyards of the admiralty on

---

[3] *Fibre & Fabric*, Vol. XXI, No. 53, May 11, 1895, "Turkish Railroads and Industries," p. 140.

the Golden Horn; while others owe their establishment to the solicitude of the Sultan for the good of his people.

"Turkish Cotton Mills.—The cotton twist manufactories of Broussa, Biledjik, Lefké, Ghemleih, Moudania and other localities in the *vilayet* of Hudavendighiar employed 10,000 workmen, and produced annually up to 2,000,000 kilogrammes of cocoons, the quality of which was; so justly valued by the silk manufacturers of Europe that they purchased them at 120 francs the kilogramme."

*Popular Science* also gave a fairly positive review.[4]

"A pamphlet entitled *A Few Facts about Turkey under the Reign of Abdul Hamid II*, by an American Observer, tells of important advances in the railroads, docks, finance, education, army, navy, and other affairs of that country. Several pages are devoted to showing that the Armenians are deceitful and conscienceless agitators. Testimony is also given to the effect that the attitude of the American missionaries towards the Armenians is not always judicious (Printed by J.J. Little & Co., New York.)."

*The Critic* also provided a favorable evaluation.[5]

"AN Anonymous Pamphlet of sixty-seven pages, entitled "A Few Facts about Turkey" (under the reign of the Sultan Abdul Hamid II.), has recently been published in New York. The author gives a striking picture of the changes wrought in the Turkish Empire as ruled by its present sovereign. He shows that considerable advance and improvement have been made in material things, but a careful reading of the pamphlet does not reveal any change of heart or improvement in moral character among the Turks. Despite the outward gloss of prosperity, there seems to be no sign of better government. He who would obtain a

---

[4] *Popular Science*, August 1895, Vol. XLVII - 35, p. 565.
[5] *The Critic*, January 25, 1896, No. 727, p. 61.

friendly view of the actual situation in the Turkish Empire should read this very strong plea of one who is an apologist for the Turks. The last eleven pages are taken up with a discussion of the Armenian outrages, the author seeking vainly to break the force of the accumulating testimony, which tends so strongly to condemn the government of the Sultan. To our mind the pamphlet contains no convincing argument to prove that the Turks really desire to govern justly, or that the hoary or thoroughly rotten system of administration can be improved by the adoption of railways, telegraphs, ironclads or repeating rifles (Privately printed)."

However, Missionary publications would deem the pamphlets to be full of lies and half-truths.

An extraordinary pamphlet has recently been issued at New York, purporting to be written by "An American Observer" entitled "A Few Facts about Turkey in the Reign of Abdul Hamid II." In this pamphlet we are told that Islamism "is indeed a religion essentially and radically tolerant." This is said in face of the notorious fact, which every Muslim in Turkey well knows, that should he profess the Christian faith his life would not be safe for a day. He must either flee or die. This pamphlet also states that "All requests for authorization to open schools presented by foreigners have always met with the best reception by the government of Abdul Hamid." Then "the best reception" of these requests must be to pigeonhole them. For long years efforts to secure official authorization for educational institutions have been met by delay after delay, and multitudes of promises made have not yet been fulfilled. A factor in the settlement of the difficulties at Marsovan some two years since, at the time of the burning of the Girls' Seminary, was the promise of a trade for Anatolia College, which promise has not teen kept. Several weeks since telegraphic announcement was made of a purpose on the part of the Turkish government to grant a petition presented long ago, for an irade for the Girls' College at

Constantinople, but at last reports the wished-for charter had not been delivered. From the time of the starting of Robert College down to the present moment those who have sought to establish educational institutions for the Christian population of Turkey have had to plead for months, and usually for years, for official permits, and many permits asked for are still withheld. "An American Observer" has in this pamphlet observed many things which are not so.[6]

From 1898 to the time of his death on October 1, 1916, Webb lived in Rutherford, New Jersey. He died at the age of seventy and was buried in Hillside Cemetery on the outskirts of Rutherford. He was survived by a son and two daughters. After Webb's death, his wife became a Unitarian and at least one daughter (Aliya) remained Muslim.

After Webb's death, his efforts were largely forgotten. There continued to exist a vague coming to Islam in the African American community and there exists some lines in the writings of the first American Islamic Nationalist, Noble Drew Ali, showing that if he hadn't met Webb at least he had heard of his efforts. For instance in the *Circle Seven Qur'an* he calls the Turks the "Saviors of Islam."[7]

This collection contains *The Armenian Troubles and Where the Responsibility Lie* and *A Few Facts about Turkey under the Reign of Abdul Hamid II*. Only minor editing to conform to American spelling for words such as honor (instead of honour), Muslim (instead of Mohammadan or Mussulman), and Islam instead of Mohammadanism were used. Only obvious spelling or punctuation errors were corrected.

Webb's other writings will be published in the forthcoming volumes: *Journals of Travels in India and the Muslim East, The Muslim World Journal – the first Muslim American magazine, Armenia and Turkey – an American Muslims View* (the current

---

[6] *The Missionary Herald* by the American Board of Commissioners for Foreign Missions, Vol. XCI, No. 5, May 1985, pp. 177-178. This review was reprinted, without change, in at least a dozen other mission oriented periodicals.

[7] "The Turks are the true descendants of Hagar, who are the chief protectors of the Islamic Creed of Mecca; beginning from Mohammed the First, the founding of the uniting of Islam, by the command of the great universal God — Allah." *Holy Koran of the Moorish Science Temple*, Chapter XLV, verse 7.

publication), and the *Journalistic Tracing of an American Muslim Editor – Webb's Journalistic Writings*. Help in finding library holding of Webb's newspapers would be greatly appreciated.

# A FEW FACTS ABOUT TURKEY

# UNDER THE REIGN OF

# ABDUL HAMID II.

By

AN AMERICAN OBSERVER

NEW YORK
1895

# A FEW FACTS ABOUT TURKEY UNDER
# THE REIGN OF ABDUL HAMID II

It is intended to give in this work a few facts showing the wonderful progress made by Turkey under its present Sultan, Abdul Hamid II. The development and advancement which has been steadily going on ever since the present Turkish sovereign ascended the imperial throne deserves to be brought before the English-speaking people.[8] In the last chapter, the author will also give his views on the Armenians and their last agitation.

## RAILWAYS

The convention of the 12th of March, 1872, had bequeathed to Turkey a system of railroads comprising the following lines:

(1) From Constantinople to Bellova, by Adrianople and Philippopolis; length, 562 kilometres.

(2) From Adrianople to Dedé-Agatch, by Kouleli-Bourgas and Demotica; length, 148 kilometres.

(3) From Salonica to Mitrovitza, by Keuprula and Uskub; length, 364 kilometres.

(4) From Yamboli to Tirnova-Semenli; length, 106 kilometres.

One must add to these three railroads in Asia:

(1) From Haïdar-Pacha to Ismit; length, 94 kilometres.

(2) From Smyrna to Aïdin; length, 507 kilometres.

(3) From Smyrna to Cassaba; length, 90 kilometres.

It belonged to the Sultan Abdul Hamid to give to the railroads of the Ottoman Empire that judicious and reasonable extension which was susceptible of contributing to the progressive development of his economical resources and of augmenting in considerable proportions his military power and his defensive strength. A simple enumeration of the railroads constructed since His Majesty ascended the throne, or which are now in construction, as well as of the concessions accorded to railroads, and which will from one moment to another be put into execution, will suffice to show how much the Ottoman Empire owes to the Sultan Abdul Hamid. If today one can go from Paris to

---

[8] The author is indebted for most of the information and statistics contained in this work to "How One Saves an Empire," a very able pamphlet on Turkish matters.

Constantinople by rail in less than four days, it is incontestably to the continued and persevering efforts of the Sultan Abdul Hamid that this great result is due. It is he who in the "Conference of Four" did not cease to insist upon the joining of the railroads of Roumelia to those of Central Europe, and the other countries must be grateful to him for the accomplishment of this great work.

The following is a schedule of the different concessions made by the Ottoman Government during the last five years:

Ismit-Angora (Anatolia RR.). (Sept. 24, Oct. 6, 1S88) 312 kilometres. The entire length of the Anatolia Road from Haïdir Pacha to Angora is 370 miles. The line is in working order from end to end.

Jaffa-Jerusalem. (Oct. 6, 1888.) 50 kilometres.

Salonica-Monastir. (Oct. 27, 1890.) 136 kilometres. The 60 kilometres which are completed were turned over Dec. 8, 1892. Everything tends to show that it will be completed when promised, April 28, 1894.

Moudania-Brousse. (Feb. 22, 1891.) 26 kilometres.

Panderma-Koniah (with branch roads). (Feb. 28, 1891.) 500 kilometres. This concession was weakened and replaced by the Allachébir-Karahissar RR.

Beyrout-Damascus-Hauran. (June 13, 1891.) 132 kilometres. In course of construction.

Samsoun-Sivas-Diarbikir. (July 2, 1891.) 750 kilometres. Not yet commenced.

St. John of Acre-Damascus. (Oct. 8-20, 1891.) 219 kilometres. Not yet commenced.

Dédé-Agatch-Salonica, with branch roads. (May 18-30, 1892.) 300 kilometres. Work was begun July 14, 1893. It is hoped to have the line completed in 1898.

Eskichéhir-Koniah. (Feb. 1-13, 1893.) 288 kilometres. Work began August 31, 1893. The length may be modified.

Angora-Césaré. (Feb. 1-13, 1893.) 256 kilometres.

Allachéhir-Karahissar. (Feb. 4, 1893.) 155 kilometres.

Damascus-Beredjik. (May 21, 1893.) 310 kilometres. The length of these last three lines may be modified when the plans are finished.

It appears that the Ismit-Angora line is actually completed and in thorough working order from beginning to end. Work on the Salonica-Monastir line has been pushed.

An old grant, that of the Panderma-Koniah Road, has been annulled and five new ones given. A word upon each of them:

(1) The Eskichéhir-Koniah Road, of an approximate length of 288 miles, is guaranteed 604 Turkish pounds per kilometre. This line is granted (leased) to the Anatolia Railroad Company, of which it is a branch. Work on this road, begun on August 31, 1893, is to be completed within four years, at the outside, after the approval of the plans.

(2) The Angora-Césaré Railroad measures about 256 miles. It has also been granted (or leased) to the Anatolia Railroad Company, of which it is an extension in the direction of Bagdad, and is guaranteed 775 Turkish pounds per kilometre. The Imperial Ottoman Government reserves the right to lessen the guarantee, but in that case the company can give up the grant. The large amount of the guarantee is explained by the technical difficulties met with in the construction of the line. The company has eight years in which to build it.

(3) The Allachéhir-Karahissar line serves as an extension to the Smyrna-Cassaba, and meets the Anatolia Railroad at Karahissar. This line will have an approximate length of 150 miles, and has an annual guarantee of 800 Turkish pounds per kilometre.

(4) The Salonica-Dédé-Agatch Railroad, of about 300 miles in length, has an annual kilometric guarantee of 15,500 francs. It makes, in connection with the Oriental railroads, direct communication between Salonica and Constantinople. The work, begun in June, 1893, is to be finished in four years.

(5) The Damascus-Beredjik line measures about 380 miles. There is attached to it an annual guarantee of 12,500 francs per kilometre. The plans have not yet been completed, and as yet no company has been formed to accept the grant.

These new grants, which cover a total in length of 1,379 miles, show the sincerity of the government in its wish to open the country to commerce and progress. At all events, it believes, and with reason, it has given sufficient guarantees for the present. There is every reason to believe that those already given will be fully paid by the receipts of the railroad.

A few figures will show what influence the opening of the railroad has had upon the economic development of the country. The tithes (in cereals) of the *Sandjak* of Angor in 1889, the year when work was begun on the Anatolia Railroad, were about 32,000 Turkish pounds, and in 1892, when about 210 miles of the line were completed, they rose to 49,000 Turkish pounds, making an increase of twenty-five percent. The *Sandjak* of Ismit, from which at the same time was received 24,000 Turkish pounds in 1889, returned 39,000 in 1892, making an increase of fifty-five percent. The tithes of the *Sandjak* of Kutathia and Erthogroul, which, although at a greater distance from the railroads, still feel their influence, have risen from 87,000 Turkish pounds in 1889 to 114,000 Turkish pounds in 1892.

This increase in the resources of the government must help considerably in the payment of the guarantees, and Mr. Vincent Cailbard has shown by figures that the year the Anatolia Railroad was opened the government received, by the augmentation of the tithes alone, a sufficient amount to pay almost one-third of their guarantee to the railroad company.

Owing to the amelioration of the conditions of the country, agriculture has been developed, a development which the government has encouraged by bringing into Turkey emigrants from Bosnia, Herzegovina, Thessaly, and the Balkan States.

The following table gives the different lines in the Ottoman Empire:

| Name of Railroads | Number miles constructed and in use |
|---|---|
| Smyrna-Adana and branches (Smyrna-Aïda Railroad) | 324.00 |
| Smyrna-Allachéhir and branches (Smyrna-Cassaba Railroad) | 165 00 |
| Moudania-Brousse | 26 00 |
| Mersina-Adana | 40 00 |
| Jaffa-Jerusalem | 53 60 |
| Salonica-Monastir | 60 00 |
| Haïdar-Pacha-Angora (Anatolia Railroad) | 370 00 |
| Constantinople-Adrianople-Moustapha-Pacha | 222 00 |
| Salonica-Uskub-Mitrovitza | 227 00 |
| Dédé-Agatch-Adrianople | 92 50 |
| Uskub-Zobeftché | 52 80 |
| | 1,632 90 |

# QUAYS

As the point of intersection of the routes which lead from Europe into Asia — key, as it were, of the routes *via* the Mediterranean, between the Occident on the one hand and Egypt and India on the other — Constantinople has been destined by nature to be one of the first commercial centres of the entire world. Therefore the concession granted for quays in 1891 was received with joy by the entire population.

What the port of Smyrna has gained by the construction of its quays — which, it can be parenthetically stated, are among the most beautiful which exist — permits us to form some idea of the profits and advantages which will be derived by the commerce of the capital in particular, and of the empire in general, by the construction of quays along the Golden Horn, for which the work is already in progress.

Simultaneously with the quays, docks are being constructed, these being the natural consequence of the former. Numbers of projects concerning great commercial storehouses have already been submitted to the Imperial Ottoman Government.

## CHAMBERS OF COMMERCE

Another most useful and important thing for which the commerce of the Ottoman Empire is also indebted to Abdul Hamid is the Ottoman Chamber of Commerce, established in 1884, at Stamboul.

On the model of the Chamber of Commerce at Constantinople, no less than one hundred and twenty-three chambers of commerce have been, up to the month of August, 1891, established in the capitals of the *vilayets*, *sandjaks*, and districts of the empire.

As a sort of annex of the Ottoman Chamber of Commerce, the Ottoman Commercial Museum, of which the establishment at Stamboul was decided by an imperial irade bearing the date of December 30, 1890, is destined also to play a great *rôle* in the commercial and industrial expansion of Turkey.

This institution will bring together, in a permanent exposition, specimens of all the agricultural and industrial productions of the empire, and both Turkish and foreign merchants will be able there to obtain valuable information relative to the nature and value of these products.

# MANUFACTORIES

In the capital and its suburbs are large industrial establishments which can defy all comparison with those of the Occident, of which some, established formerly, have received from the incessant care and attention of the Sultan a second life, as it were. Such are the manufactory of the military cloths of Fezhané; the superb workshops of the "Grande Maîtrise" of Artillery at Tophané and the dockyards of the Admiralty on the Golden Horn; while others owe their establishment to the solicitude of the Sultan for the good of his people.

These latter are: the manufactory of the administration of tobaccos, at Djubali, Stamboul (1884), which employs fifteen hundred workers of both sexes, and of which the production goes up as high as three million Turkish pounds annually; the manufactory of cement at Kiretch-Bournou (1891); the manufactory of the Ottoman Thread and Cotton Company, at Yedi-Koulé (1890); the gas-works of the new Stamboul Gas Company, at Yedi-Koulé (also 1891); the new railroad station of the Oriental Railroad at Sirkedji (Stamboul), inaugurated in 1891; the glass-works at Tchebouklou, and those of artificial ice at Stenia (Bosphorus), etc.

# IMPROVEMENTS AT CONSTANTINOPLE

Gardens have been made at Yildiz, at Péra, at Taxim, at Stamboul, at Scutari, and a zoölogical and botanical garden has been founded.

Péra no longer dreads the lack of water, since the "Dercos-Waters" Company (1886) conducts to its inhabitants that indispensable element to all agglomerations of individuals, not only for personal use, but for public hygiene.

Stamboul will also find itself thus provided when the "Dercos-Waters" Company, which has also obtained the concession for supplying water to that part of the capital, will have finished — and this will be soon — its work of canalization.

The Tramway Company has added, in 1885, a new line to its system, which runs between Galata and Chichli, to the great satisfaction of all the proprietors in these quarters of this suburb of Péra, whose estates have suddenly acquired a great value.

The new Stamboul Gas Company furnishes to the prefectorate of the city, as well as to individuals, lighting at better terms than formerly, and the government expects, and is exerting itself at present, to improve the system of gas-lighting at Péra.

Scutari, which, though on the Asiatic shore, must be considered a third part of the capital, has nothing to envy in Stamboul or Péra in the way of water or gas. The concessionary water company has commenced to place its conduits, and the gas company, of which the works are now being constructed at Courbaghili-Déré, is taking measures to establish at Scutari a reservoir containing three thousand cubic metres. The same advantages will be enjoyed by Cadikeny, the ancient Chalcedon.

## NEW ENTERPRISES AT SALONICA, SMYRNA, AND BEYROUT AND OTHER PLACES

Among other improvements of which Salonica has been the recipient, said city is lighted by gas since 1889, and the concessionary water company commenced its work some two years ago. The canalization of the Vardar, for which all the plans have been made, will beautify and sanitize the city. And, lastly, Salonica will also have quays which will in no way be surpassed by those of Smyrna or Constantinople.

At Smyrna commerce has become so developed that the Hamidié Ottoman Navigation Company no longer suffices to the requirements, more and more exigent, of this port. Two new companies, the Chirket Sultané and the Chirket Hamidié, will do the duty of the coasting trade in the Gulf of Smyrna and the neighboring sea-ports.

The canalization of the Hermus (Meander), in putting the salt-pits of Phocaea and the plain of, Menemen out of the reach of the inundations of the stream, will greatly increase the returns of these valuable salt-pits, and of that plain of which the poets have sung, from the most ancient times to our own days, in praise of its inexhaustible fertility.

Beyrout, that central supply station of Syria, has been transformed as though by enchantment, by the lighting of it by gas (1884-1885); by the making of a port, for which the concession was granted in 1888, and of which the construction is being methodically

21

pursued; as well as by an uninterrupted and regular distribution of the water necessary to its inhabitants.

Water, that element so highly to be appreciated in all hot climates such as Syria, will now continuously render fruitful the plain of Jaffa, and transform its sands into a verdant garden.

Inéboli, on the Black Sea, continues the construction of its quays, commenced by the government itself.

The manufactory of *etrété* cloths in the neighborhood of Ismit, now entirely reorganized and possessed of perfected machinery, gives to the market stuffs justly estimated and of which the reputation augments annually, for which impulse gratitude is due to the Sultan Abdul Hamid.

Similarly, the Marine Arsenal at Ismit, so marvelously situated at the head of the bay of Nicomedia, has become one of the principal dockyards of the Ottoman war marine, temporarily, till the establishment of a military port which will defy all attacks.

The coal basin of Heraclea, which had been abandoned, notwithstanding that it contained in the profundities of its soil inexhaustible treasures of pit coal, is once more, by the foresight of the Sultan, in active exploitation.

The copper mines of Arghana and the auriferous and argentiferous lead mines of Bulgar-Dagh have nearly doubled their production.

The bituminous mines of Selenitza, vilayet of Janina, already vie with European products, and in a near future will, indeed, quite crowd out the latter from Turkish markets.

Native societies have been formed which advantageously exploit, with perfected machines and of the latest model, these mines, notably so rich in borax, copper, argentiferous lead, chrome magnesia, and emery.

Dikes and causeways have been constructed along the Bayana and the Drin in Albania.

## INCREASING THE COMMERCIAL IMPORTANCE
## OF CONSTANTINOPLE

It is necessary to mention, also, with considerable detail, as it is destined to exercise a most considerable influence on the commercial future of the port of Constantinople, an undertaking which is due exclusively to the Sultan Abdul Hamid.

This is the regulation of the course of the Euphrates, of which the civil list has borne all the expense.

It was question of establishing a double service of steamboats — the one on the Tigris and the Chatt-el-Arab, between Mossul (Asia Minor), Bagdad, and Bassorah; the other on the Euphrates and the Chatt-el-Arab, between Meskené and Bassorah. The first part of the undertaking offered no great difficulties; but in order that the steamers of the Meskené-Bassorah line could ply regularly between these two cities, it was necessary to reconstruct, as it were, all that part of the Euphrates comprised between Hindich and Sanunaroa. For a length of 150 kilometres the river is almost always dry in summer, the waters flowing off into the Hindich Canal. In the space of a year, from October 1, 1890, to October 9, 1891, the river had been brought back into its ancient bed. A lock formed by 30,000 cubic feet of rock, stones, and bricks compels the Euphrates to follow its normal bed and course, leaving only sufficient water for the supply of the Hindich Canal. The immediate result of these works was to save from inundations the beautiful palm plantations of the *Sandjak* of Hille; but this result is trifling if compared to the commercial supremacy attained in consequence by Constantinople. Joined to the navigable waters of the Euphrates, which commence at Beredjik, Constantinople is in a position now to vie advantageously with the Suez Canal, not only in regard to merchandise, but also in regard to the transportation of passengers, as it is the key of the most direct route between the Occident and the extreme Orient. In a few years Constantinople will be key to the traffic of all the valley of the Euphrates and the Tigris, as well as that part of Persia which is contiguous. These inestimable advantages are, by the regulation of the course of the Euphrates, insured to Turkey.

## COTTON MILLS

The cotton-twist manufactories of Broussa, Biledjik, Lefké, Ghemleih, Moudania, and other localities in the vilayet of Hudavendighiar, employed 10,000 workmen and produced annually up to 2,000,000 kilogrammes of cocoons, the quality of which was so justly valued by the silk manufacturers of Europe that they purchased them at 120 francs the kilogramme.

## CULTIVATION OF SILK-WORMS

Since then, in consequence of one of those natural causes which outweigh all human calculations — the silk-worm plague, of which the first appearance at the vilayet of Hudavendighiar dates back thirty-five years, a plague which science was then impotent in combating — the culture of the silk-worm had declined to the degree that the production of cocoons had fallen to the low estimate of only 400,000 kilogrammes. The mulberry-tree plantations had been in great part destroyed and the factories closed. It is for this reason that the Sultan decreed, *proprio motu*, the preparation of cellular grains of silk-worms, in accordance with the system of Pasteur. This measure saved the culture of the silk-worm from annihilation, as may be seen by the fact that in the year 1892 the production of cocoons in the vilayet of Hudavendighiar reached 1,700,000 kilogrammes, and this upward impetus can only follow an arithmetical progression.

It may be added here that in order to prevent any internal shackles from hindering the progress of Ottoman commerce and industry, of which his high and distinguished experience warned him, the Sultan decreed, two years ago, the abolition of internal customs which fettered the transportation of products from one vilayet to another, allowing to remain only a tax of ten percent on foreign merchandise imported or in transit through the empire, and on merchandise of native production destined for exportation.

## AGRICULTURAL BANK

Today, thanks to the Sultan Abdul Hamid, who instituted the Agricultural Bank, the peasant is freed from the claws of the usurers. In 1883 the attention of his Imperial Majesty was attracted by this deplorable situation, and, from that, developed in his mind the thought which was to express itself by the establishment, so propitious, of the Agricultural Bank. The old provincial savings-banks formed their capital by means of the result of the sale of provisions and products of all kinds, economized by the agricultural population in excess of the harvest, and placed at their disposal. This payment in kind is now replaced, at the Agricultural Bank, by a surtax of two percent on all tithes. When the capital of the bank will, however, have attained a certain sum, enabling it to meet with assurance all the possible exigencies of the future, then reimbursement will be made to those who contributed to this surtax. The Agricultural Bank lends at six percent, plus one percent for registry, sums varying from the smallest possible to 150 Turkish pounds, for a time extending from three to ten years. This bank receives also deposits, on which it pays four percent annual interest. At Stamboul is the central administration; at the chief towns of vilayets are annex offices; at the chief towns of sandjaks are agencies, and at the chief towns of cantons, offices. Each annex office or agency obtains its resources from the contributions of agriculturists in its radius, and lends to none but these.

The following article, taken from the "Journal of the Chamber of Commerce of Constantinople," dated April 7, 1894, will be found interesting:

"The Chamber of Commerce of Agriculture and of Industry of Constantinople has just received a notice of the balance sheet and of the report of the operations of the Agricultural Bank during the financial year 1307 (that is to say, for the space of time comprised between the 1st of March, 1891, and the 29th of February, 1892).

"We hasten to place under the eyes of our readers the figures of this balance sheet referring to an institution in which we have, since its creation, felt a lively interest.

"Since the time of its foundation the Directors and the Managing Board of this Bank have shown the greatest activity, and have given proofs of an intelligence and technical knowledge which have placed the bank on an equal footing with the best foreign institutions of a similar character.

"It is true that the rural banks founded on the system of Raifeisen and others, to be found scattered over Germany, Russia, Italy, France, and other countries, are aiming at spreading through all classes of the rural population the benefits of agricultural credit; but the Agricultural Ottoman Bank is invested today with an organization and management which are peculiar to it, and which might serve, with a few modifications of detail, as a model for other countries. The honor of this fact is incontestably due to our Sovereign, His Imperial Majesty the Sultan Abdul Hamid II.

"At present the Agricultural Bank has 95 branch offices and 328 agencies in the different parts of the Ottoman Empire; three of these branch offices and twenty-three of these agencies were established in the course of the year 1307.

"The capital of this institution amounted, at the close of the year 1360, to 291,941,946 piastres. This capital was increased in the following manner by 63,786,930 piastres, of which 42,049,856 were proceeds from the tax of public instruction, and returnable to the Bank; 5,060,701 being the product of interest accrued in favor of the Bank; 644,858 the product of the registration fee; and the rest, about 16,032,015 piastres, Being the proceeds of the credits of the public banks which were suppressed. The capital thus was estimated at 355,733,876 piastres.

"As regards expenses, the total amount expended during the year 1307 was 10,898,820 piastres; of this total, 4,872,175 piastres represent the total working expenses of the Bank, which amount is very moderate, considering the number of branch offices and agencies, and the complication of the service; 1,286,878 piastres were expended for the benefit of the agricultural interests; 2,848,354 piastres for roads and highways and for the agricultural inspectors; and 1,890,418 for different other needs.

"During the year 1307 a total of 60,760,013 piastres were loaned to cultivators, which, added to the amount of accepted loans accepted during the preceding transactions of the Bank, raises the amount of sums loaned by the Bank during the space of two years to 117,386,219 piastres. From its establishment to the end of the year 1307, that is to say, during three years, the Agricultural Bank loaned 123,768,955 piastres to cultivators, which represents a very important service rendered to agriculture, especially in those localities where entire families were being ruined for having had in times of distress the imprudence to borrow only 100 piastres from the usurers. The capital of the Agricultural Bank having, as above stated, been increased by 63,786,930 piastres in 1307, the accepted loans during the same year, of about 60,760,012 piastres, have then equaled the first sum, which proves indisputably that the work of assimilation and non-assimilation is regularly carried on in the working of this institution, enjoying perfect conditions of viability. It is true that, compared to the nominal capital of 344,000,000 of piastres disposed of by the Bank up to the close of the year 1307, the total of the accepted loans may appear absurd; but one must bear in mind that the realizable portion of this loan is reduced only to 143,000,000, of which 25,000,000, representing the tithes on the tax of public instruction, would only be banked in the course of the year 1308. 13,600,000 piastres were retained by superior order as a reserve fund. As to the balance, say 105,000,000 of piastres, which represents the entire fund at the disposal of the Agricultural Bank fund, more than 90,000,000 piastres were applied to the accepted loans, and the remaining 10,500,000 piastres compose the amount banked by the branch offices and agencies, which scarcely makes an average deposit of 25,000 per agency.

"In the interest of national agriculture the following sums have been expended:

|  | Piastres |
|---|---|
| School of Agriculture of Halkali | 246,093 13 |
| School of Agriculture Salonica | 260,588 32 |
| School of Agriculture Broussa | 291,118 39 |
| Model Farm of Angora | 61,184 00 |
| Model Farm of Adama | 32,560 00 |
| Model Farm of Erzeroum | 9,376 27 |
| Model Farm of Alep | 71,354 25 |
| Model Farm of Sevas | 27,132 15 |
| Model Farm of Damascus | 40,951 10 |
| Model Farm of Konich | 58,092 30 |

"Expenses of instruction for fourteen students sent to France to study agriculture 130,919 14

"Seeds purchased in Europe and in America for distribution to farmers                                          72,794 00

"Cost of 1000 thermometers for distribution to silkworm raisers                                                        2,250 00

"Paid by General Board of Administration for the destruction of grasshoppers which were devastating the fields of Kutchuk Tchekmedje, and for the municipal circumscriptions of the III and IV circles          3,325 00

-----------------------

Total 1,307,741 05

"Independently of this sum, the General Board of Directors authorized the branch offices to open a supplementary fund of 251,700 piastres for the work of destroying the grasshoppers.

"Inspectors nominated during the year 1308 to assure the effective working of the service, having visited the majority of the branch offices and agencies, have reported that the most perfect regularity was observed in the service of loans and other portions of the system. But these inspectors having reported that a few of the employees had been guilty of certain abuses prejudicial to the borrowers, these employees were discharged from office and punished according to law. In order that this measure might serve as a good example to others, it was decided to publish in full the names of the delinquent employees, stating the cause of their dismissal, and to transmit a copy of this statement to each branch office and agency.

"With a view of preventing the authorities of the branch offices and agencies from taking advantage of the ignorance of the borrowers as regards the law concerning these transactions, it was also arranged to give the greatest publicity to the most trivial charges in the regulation of the Bank, through the medium of public posters couched in terms entirely comprehensible to all classes of the community.

"Moreover, in consideration of the fact that the borrowers lose much time by being obliged to return to their villages in order to rectify errors which frequently occur in one drawing of the certificates which they have delivered to them by the *moukhtars* in order to substantiate their standing as farmers, it has been decided to have printed, under the care of the general direction, certificates of this kind, and to cause them to be distributed among the *moukhtars*, to be delivered to those whom they may concern. At the foot of these certificates are also set forth the necessary instructions as to the most minute formalities to be observed in borrowing from the Agricultural Bank.

"A fact worthy of remark is the daily habit which the population has of depositing money in the Bank, which, as we know, allows an interest of four percent to its depositors. During the year 1307, these deposits amounted to the sum of $362,272.37 \,^{50/100}$ piastres, which is in itself a fair encouragement for a commencement, especially so in places where saving is not a general practice. The Bank has paid from this source, and from the source of interest accruing from accepted loans amongst the agencies, a total amounting to 44,295 piastres.

"Among the real estate properties which the Bank has secured the right to sell at public auction in order to assure the return of its loans, of which the value has amounted to 307,805.14 piastres, country property to the amount of 292,031.39 piastres have been transferred, for want of a higher bidder, to the credit of the Agricultural Bank.

"During the year 1307 the Agricultural Bank has taken the delivery of farm products, to the value of 2,077,405.15 piastres, from the head tax collector, in the shape of taxes which were due to it. Of these products there have been sold 994,310.04 piastres' worth, and the residue remains in the custody of the Bank.

"On the other hand, there have been expended in the year 1307, 2,615,462.26 piastres for legal expenses, retainers, and other fees, a total of which a portion, say as much as 741,364 piastres, had been for one reason or another defrayed by the Bank, and the rest has been charged against the borrowers, who owed already to this fund, from the year 1306, a sum of 87,819.22 piastres.

"Over and above these operations the Agricultural Bank has effected collections and payments on the part of the Minister of Public Instruction, and for that of Finance by reason of the collection of taxes of prestation for the construction of roads and highways,

"An imperial *irade* having authorized the general direction of the Agricultural Bank to increase its budget of expenses, the increase of the staff of officers and that of emoluments will allow of the drawing up each year of the balance sheet of annual operations."

## AGRICULTURAL SCHOOLS

The agricultural schools of Turkey are, since 1891, four in number: one at Halkali, near Stamboul; others at Smyrna, Beyrout, and Broussa.

To each one of these schools is annexed a model farm, so that practical instruction goes hand in glove with theoretic instruction, and one helps to demonstrate the other. Independently of the model farms annexed to the agricultural schools, there are other establishments which render to agriculture signal services. They are those of the Crown domains, of which each one is a model farm and leaves nothing to be desired.

## FORESTRY

Sylviculture, that department of agriculture which appertains particularly to the culture of forest trees, belongs to the agricultural system of a country, of which it constitutes one of the most productive branches. The Sultan Abdul Hamid has again in this department been a creator and organizer, for it is from his reign that dates the Ottoman Forestry Department. In this department Turkey has nothing to envy other nations, thanks to the measures adopted for the prevention of cutting down of trees and also preventing coal-men and shepherds from devastating a whole forest in order to obtain a few tons of coal, or arrange a pasture ground for their herds.

In Turkey the forests occupy a surface of 15,955,192 *deneums* — that is, in the neighborhood of a twenty-fourth part of the territory of the Ottoman Empire — and in this are only comprised the *vilayets* of European Turkey, Anatolia, and Anterior Asia. Fifteen varieties of trees, each one more useful than the other to industry, compose these forests. Among the principal varieties are the oak, the walnut, the maple, the poplar, the pine, the plane-tree, the lime-tree, the chestnut, the palm, and the olive-tree. In the future the Ottoman Empire, which is so rich in precious woods of every kind to supply the markets of Europe, will be in a position to derive profitable advantage, in favor of the imperial treasury, out of this natural fortune, which remained, up to the present reign, in stagnation so complete as to render it unproductive.

## DEPARTMENT OF AGRICULTURE, OF MINES, AND OF FORESTRY

The following gives a comparative table of the receipts of Mines and Forestry during the year 1309 (1893-1894), which terminated on March 1-13, 1894, and during the year 1308 (1892-1893), showing in the receipts, or revenues, of 1309 (1893-1894), a surplus of more than 47 percent — that is, 11,625,282 piastres in Lt. 116,000, of which 47,459 is derived from the Forestry, 9,600 from rights on mines, and 59,180 from receipts of mines exploited by the State.

The brilliant result showed constitutes the best praise on the establishment of a Department (or Ministry) of Agriculture, of Mines, and Forestry, which every one knows is due to the initiative taken by the Sultan Abdul Hamid.

# RECEIPTS TAKEN IN

## ON THE PRECEDING YEARS
| | |
|---|---|
| From March 1$^{st}$ to end of February, 1309 | 7,864,793 07 |
| From March 1$^{st}$ to end of February, 1308 | 3,690,611 26 |
| Surplus in favor of 1309 | 4,174,181 21 |

## ANNO 1309
| | |
|---|---|
| From March 1$^{st}$ to end of February, 1309 | 25,003,531 06 |
| From March 1$^{st}$ to end of February, 1308 | 20,149,605 30 |
| Surplus in favor of 1309 | 4,823,925 16 |

## TOTAL
| | |
|---|---|
| From March 1$^{st}$ to end of February, 1309 | 32,868,324 13 |
| From March 1$^{st}$ to end of February, 1308 | 23,840,217 16 |
| Surplus in favor of 1309 | 8,028,106 37 |

# RECEIPTS VERIFIED

## ON THE PRECEDING YEARS
| | |
|---|---|
| From March 1$^{st}$ to end of February, 1309 | 9,227,430 31 |
| From March 1$^{st}$ to end of February, 1308 | 2,289,595 34 |
| Surplus in favor of 1309 | 6,397,834 37 |

## ANNO 1309
| | |
|---|---|
| From March 1$^{st}$ to end of February, 1309 | 26,780,367 05 |
| From March 1$^{st}$ to end of February, 1308 | 21,552,919 24 |
| Surplus in favor of 1309 | 5,227,447 21 |

## TOTAL
| | |
|---|---|
| From March 1$^{st}$ to end of February, 1309 | 36,007,797 36 |
| From March 1$^{st}$ to end of February, 1308 | 24,382,515 18 |
| Surplus in favor of 1309 | 11,625,282 18 |

|  | Piastres |
|---|---|
| Surplus of first six months | 4,817,683 33 |
| Surplus of second six months | 6,807,598 25 |
| Total | 11,625,282 18 |

## REDIVISION OF SURPLUS

|  | Piastres |
|---|---|
| Forestry revenues | 4,745,969 06 |
| Mines exploited by the state | 5,918,981 22 |
| Mines in concession | 900,331 30 |
| Total | 11,625,282 18 |

|  | Piastres |
|---|---|
| Payments made at the Ministry of Finance in 1308 | 12,389,401 17 |
| Payments made at the Ministry of Finance in 1309 | 16,995,242 28 |
|  | 4,605,841 11 |

Thus in 1309 there is a surplus of 47 percent, with reference to the year 1308 (1892-1893), which latter year represented the largest receipts received until then.

## CREDIT IMMOBILIER

By one of those happy inspirations which belong to the Sultan, the "Credit Immobilier" established itself in the most simple fashion, without those who contributed to it having any burden to carry, and without having to dread those fluctuations of speculation of which one has seen so many sad examples in Europe.

While preserving its original character, the Savings-Bank of Constantinople is authorized to consent to loans on real- estate mortgages. Instead of investing those funds which are entrusted to it in stocks, which are always more or less uncertain, it invests them in real estate, which represents a certainty, and escapes more than any other investment from sudden depreciations which, without apparent or even real cause, so greatly affect other investments. At present the capital of the "Credit Immobilier" is fixed at 1,000,000 Turkish pounds, of which 450,000 pounds are furnished by the Civil Pension Bank and the rest by the State Lottery. This capital will be gradually increased, according to necessity, up to the sum of 2,000,000 Turkish pounds.

## TURKISH DEBT

Negotiations, conducted with an integrity to which the creditors of Turkey were pleased to render homage, and a skill which partook of the miraculous, brought about a settlement of the Turkish debt on December 20, 1881. At this time the entire debt of Turkey amounted to 254,292,000 pounds sterling. The loans of the preceding reigns (from 1858 to 1875), including the loan of Turkish shares at a premium — capitalization of a yearly revenue of 14,000 francs per kilometre of railroads to be constructed in the Ottoman Empire by the grantee of the Roumelian Railroad — constituted a total of 218,430,510 pounds sterling. On that sum, up to the moment of the suspension of payment of the coupon, there had been redeemed 25,947,825 pounds sterling, which reduced the figures to 192,488,625 pounds sterling. But in consequence of the addition of 61,803,915 pounds sterling, representing the arrears of interest clue since September, 1875, the general debt reached, on the 20th of December, 1881, the amount, above mentioned, of 254,292,000 pounds sterling.

To the general debt must be added besides:

(1) A sum of 8,590,000 Turkish pounds, representing different loans contracted with the bankers of Galata, before 1880, for pressing needs of the treasury, as collateral for which the Imperial Ottoman Government had, by the convention of November 22nd, ceded to its creditors the revenues from salt, tobacco, spirits, stamps, silk, and fisheries.

(2) The war indemnity due to Russia in virtue of the treaty of peace, amounting probably to 802,500,000 francs.

(3) The indemnity due to Russian merchants injured by the war of 1877-78, probably amounting to 26,750,000 francs.

The aim of the convention of December 20, 1881, was not to deal with the claims which Russia might have against Turkey, as the treaty of Berlin expressly stipulated that these were covered by the stocks of the Ottoman bondholders. It was therefore merely a question of the general debt. The arrangement comprised two entirely distinct parts: the debt proper — that is to say, the loans contracted in 1858, 1860, 1862, 1863, 1865, 1867, 1872, and 1875 — and the Turkish shares. The debt proper was subdivided in the following manner:

(1) 186,756,510 pounds sterling, being the total of these eight loans, from which were to be deducted 18,932,060 pounds sterling for the different redemptions effected up to the suspension of payment, and a further deduction of 8,668,450 pounds sterling, being at that time in the treasury, which brought the capital loaned to 159,156,000 pounds sterling.

(2) The amount of the provisional bonds, called *"Ramazan"* delivered as representing half the interest and the redemption for the amount due in September, 1875, according to the imperial irade of October 6, 1875 (6$^{th}$ *Ramazan*, 1292), *viz.*: 1,829,685 pounds sterling.

This general total of 160,985,688 pounds sterling was reduced to 92,225,827 pounds sterling, being an allowance for Turkey of 42.71 percent on the original capital. The general debt, thus brought back to 92,225,827 pounds sterling, yielded an interest of one per cent, per annum, and was in a position to be raised progressively, and according to circumstances, to four percent The Turkish bonds were subdivided into 1,980,000 shares of 400 francs each, bearing an annual interest of three percent, redeemable in 104 years by six annual drawings, on the 1$^{st}$ of February, April, June, August, October, and December of each year. Up to the 1st of October, 1875, inclusive, there had been redeemed 11,000 shares, at 400 francs, or 4,440,000 francs, or 177,600 pounds sterling, of which remained a balance of 31,512,400 pounds sterling in circulation. By the settlement of December 20, 1881, each share of 400 francs was reduced 45.09 percent, and was worth 180 francs and 36 centimes in its new form. The new capital of Turkish bonds was fixed at 14,211,406 pounds sterling. The Turkish bonds between two decrees, bonds issued at a premium and redeemable from the time of the drawing of October 1, 1875, until that of December 1$^{st}$, inclusive, amounted to 15,350 shares, representing a nominal capital of 28,180,000 francs. They carried with them the right of a previous deduction of twenty-five percent of the annuity accruing to the Turkish shares from the time of resumption of payments, and to the amount of twenty percent of the sums bearing premium and redeemed. The payment of the interest of the Turkish shares was suspended and was not to be resumed until there should remain a surplus over and above the sum necessary to meet the whole demand of premiums, in which case the interest would be payable with the bonds proceeding from the drawing. There were then appropriated to the service of the debt thus reduced the following revenues, which the Imperial Ottoman Government conceded to its creditors in order that they might manage them themselves:

(a) The six indirect imposts or taxes on salt, tobacco, spirits, stamps, silk, and fisheries, which the bankers of Galata reconveyed to the bearers of the Ottoman bonds.

(b) The excess of the custom dues resulting from the change of the rate of taxes, in case of the revision of the commercial regulations.

The Department of the Ottoman Public Debt will be benefited by this increase:

(c) The increase of revenues accruing from the general application of the law concerning patents compared with the previous receipts from the taxation of the "*Temettu.*"

(d) The tribute from the principality of Bulgaria until such time as the signing powers of the treaty of Berlin should have fixed the amount, by an annual allotment of 100,000 Turkish pounds, to be taken from the tax on tobacco.

If after the tribute or tax was fixed the Sublime Porte deemed it proper to employ it wholly or in part in some other way, the amount thus withdrawn from the bondholders was to be replaced by a sum equal to the tax on tobacco; or, in case of the insufficiency of this resource, from any other revenue equally safe.

(e) The excess from the revenues of the island of Cyprus, replaced, in case it should not prove at the disposal of the Ottoman Imperial Government, by an annual sum of 100,000 Turkish pounds, to be deducted from the tax on tobacco after the liquidation of the 100,000 Turkish pounds substituted to the share of Bulgaria. In case of this surplus not being sufficient to complete the 130,000 pounds, the general Department of Customs was to remit half-yearly drafts equivalent to the difference.

(f) The indebtedness of Eastern Roumelia, fixed at 240,000 Turkish pounds per annum, plus the net annual revenue of the customs of the province, valued at 5,000 Turkish pounds.

(g) The revenue of the *tumbeki*, to the amount of 50,000 Turkish pounds, secured by the half-yearly drafts on the general Department of Customs.

(h) All sums coming to the Imperial Turkish Government as contributive parts — from Serbia, Montenegro, Bulgaria, and Greece — of the national Ottoman debt, in accordance with the stipulation of the treaties of Berlin and the convention of Constantinople of May 24, 1881.

As has been said above, the six indirect taxes figuring in paragraph (a) were pledged to the bankers of Galata, creditors of the Imperial Ottoman Empire for a sum of 8,590,000 Turkish pounds. By an agreement between the interested parties, a covenant was agreed upon on December 28, 1881, by which the bankers transferred the management of the six contributions to the public treasury in consideration of the receipt of 371,363 shares of 22 Turkish pounds each, bearing interest of five per cent, per annum, representing a capital of 8,169,986 Turkish pounds. These shares had a right of priority over all the other loans of the Ottoman public debt, which appropriated to them a sum of 590,000 Turkish pounds for interest and redemption, to be deducted each year by privilege from the clear product of the six indirect imposts. That is why these shares bear the name of Priorities. This convention of December 20, 1881, was to be fruitful in results favorable to the increase of the finances of the Ottoman Empire, not only by the immediate advantages which it gave, but by the future contingencies which it rendered possible. In the wisdom of its author, the Sultan Abdul Hamid, the imperial *irade* of December, 1881, had laid down the principle for a conversion of the Ottoman public debt which consolidated it for the greatest benefit of all public transactions and of the service of the great book.

The syndicates of the financial establishments of London, Paris, Vienna, and Berlin, representing a great majority of the holders of Ottoman bonds, did not hesitate to adopt this view. An imperial irade, dated July 31, 1883, sanctioned the project of the conversion of the reduced public debt presented by this directing council of conceded revenues, and authorized the issue of new stock. The latter operations took place on May 13, 1884, and the delegates of the control of the conversion having been appointed on July 23rd following, operations commenced on November 20th. The positive closing of them was fixed from May 1 to May 13, 1888. But this conversion, or, more properly speaking, this consolidation, of the new Ottoman public debt was only the preliminary of other conventions which, while reducing still further the capital of the general debt and of the floating interior debt, were to furnish important sums to the Imperial Ottoman treasury. Such have been the conversion of the priority obligation and of the Defense Loan. An imperial irade, dated April 27, 1890, decreed the issuing of a loan of privileged conversion, at four percent, of 195,681,500 francs, guaranteed by the revenues of the public debt, for the conversion or the reimbursement, according to the will of the holders, of five percent obligations of priority on the same revenues. This loan was divided into 391,363 shares of 500 francs, to bearer, yielding twenty francs per annum, and payable at par in forty-four years, or in eighty-eight half-yearly drawings, effected at Constantinople in February and August of each year, under the surveillance of the directing council of the public debt and the Imperial Ottoman Bank. The interest was payable half-yearly in gold, on March 13th and September 13th, in Paris, Constantinople, London, Berlin, Frankfort, and Amsterdam, in the offices of the Ottoman Bank or those of its agents. The price of issue was fixed at 411 francs 50 centimes from March 13, 1890. The holders of five percent bonds of priority were entitled to subscribe by privilege and without reduction to the new stock, free titles, at the rate of 110 francs. The annuity appertaining to the five percent priority bonds, which were to be entirely redeemed in 1906, was, in accordance with the convention of December 20, 1881, the amount of 537,000 pounds sterling. The new issue bearing an annuity of 392,000 pounds sterling, there resulted an allowance of 145,000 pounds sterling per annum, which was appropriated to the redemption of the four series of the general debt in equal proportions, except for the first, which only received 10,000 pounds sterling. If this conversion of the priorities had been limited to this, it would not, however advantageous it might have been for the situation of the public debt in Turkey, have been of any direct benefit to the Ottoman treasury. Here it was that the financial ability of the Sultan Abdul Hamid showed itself in a most striking manner, by causing the bearers of the floating home debt ("*Sehims*," "*Moukata*," "*Istikrazi*") to profit by this operation. The financial syndicate which had taken charge of the conversion of the priorities took upon itself a loan of five million of Turkish pounds, in shares bearing four percent interest and one percent redemption fees. Of this amount, 2,500,000 Turkish pounds were devoted to the conversion of the "*Sehims*" and of the "*Moukata*," etc.; 100,000 Turkish pounds were appropriated to the settling of certain liabilities of the Imperial Ottoman treasury. As to the balance of the issue, say, 1,500,000

Turkish pounds, it was taken steadily by the syndicate, at the rate, for the total issue, of 75, which gave about 1,100,000 Turkish pounds into the state treasury. On June 3, 1890, an official notice in the Turkish newspapers of Constantinople defined the condition of the conversion of a portion of the bonds of the floating debt. The *"Sehims"* — that is, *"Mutébellé"* (converted); that is, *"Djedidiés"* (new); that is, *"Aidé"* (ordinaries) — the *"Moukata,"* and the *"Istikrazi Bahile Tahvilati"* (home loan contracted during and after the Turco-Russian war), were to be exchanged for the new bonds, payable to bearer, called Turkish bonds.

The amount of the convertible capital was fixed as follows:

(1) For the converted and new *"Sehims,"* at a sum equal to ten years of interest, calculated at the rate fixed for these securities.

(2) For the ordinary *"Sehims"* and for the *"Moukata,"* at a sum equal to eight years of interest.

(3) For the home debt, on the basis of the existing capital.

In 1891 arose a new combination, which is still a subject of study, and from which, if it be realized, much is to be hoped for in favor of the Ottoman Empire's finances. It is a matter of the capitalization of the 145,000 pounds sterling saved annually for the conversion of the priorities. There will be created by the aid of this annuity a new loan of 2,900,000 pounds sterling in Ottoman priority shares of the same standard as that of April 27 — that is to say, at four per cent, interest and one percent redemption, payable in forty-four years.

The C and D series of the Ottoman debt being quoted lower than the two first series, it was natural that the effort of supplementary redemption should bear on them. With this aim, the syndicate which was to take firm hold of the new lot of Ottoman priorities at 80 pledged itself to deliver as payment shares of the series C and D. At the price which these shares commanded at that time, which moreover did not vary for an effective capital of 2,320,000 pounds sterling, there would be withdrawn from circulation 11,600,000 pounds sterling of the general debt. Now, these 11,600,000 pounds sterling bearing the one per cent, by virtue of the convention of December 20, 1881 — that is to say, 116,000 pounds sterling — the service of the Ottoman public debt would find itself, thanks to the capitalization of the 145,000 pounds sterling, relieved from an annual claim of 116,000 pounds sterling. This operation is so important that the government of the

Sultan Abdul Hamid will take no hasty resolution in the matter, and will only decide with a thorough knowledge of its peculiarities, after having well weighed all considerations.

The Turkish shares have also profited in a notable manner from the advantages accruing from the conversion of the shares of priority. The redemption of these shares amounted to from fifty-eight percent to seventy-two percent. Thus, the winner of the capital prize of the lottery of 600,000 francs, instead of receiving 348,000 francs, as has been the case until now, will henceforth receive 422,000 francs.

Let us now consider the conversion of the Defense Loan by means of the capitalization of a portion of the Egyptian tax. In 1887 the government of the Sultan had thought of converting the different loans guaranteed by this tax which Egypt pays to the Sublime Porte. Different circumstances, both political and financial, hindered the immediate conclusion of this operation. But as soon as the Sultan saw the propitious moment, he resumed, in 1891, the execution of his plans, and his efforts were crowned by complete success. Issued in 1887, the Defense Loan, the last loan guaranteed by this Egyptian tax, amounted to 5,000,000 pounds sterling, bearing five percent interest and one percent redemption. In February, 1891, during the preliminary negotiations between the Imperial Ottoman Government and the financial syndicate, the operation of the redemption fund had reduced the original amount of the loan to 4,316,520 pounds sterling. Of the annuity of 280,622 pounds sterling which this loan guaranteed, the imperial *irade* of March 2, 1891, referring to the conversion of the Defense Loan, deducted 1,403 pounds sterling for expenses and commission, and 20,543 pounds sterling for the purpose of redemption, leaving thus an annual sum of 252,676 pounds sterling to capitalize, say at four percent — a nominal sum of 6,316,930 pounds sterling. At the price of issue of 90, this nominal capital gave a real capital of 5,685,237 pounds sterling, which the reduction of the commission of one per cent, warrantors on the nominal capital brought back to the net sum of 5,622,068 pounds sterling. Of this sum, the conversion at par of the existing bonds of the Defense Loan absorbed 4,316,530 pounds sterling. From which there is for the imperial treasury a net gain of 1,305,538 pounds sterling. This certainly is a handsome result, which has no need of comment to be appreciated at its just value by the reader.

In order to complete this rapid review of the conversions of the present Ottoman loans, there remains only to speak of a project which, decided in principle, doubtless will not be long in becoming an accomplished fact.

It is an issue of a loan of 5,000,000 pounds sterling, bearing interest at three per cent, and a redemption of one percent, which would enable the Imperial Ottoman Government to buy back the loan of the consolidation (union of the railroads of Roumelia with those of Central Europe), amounting to 810,000 pounds sterling, and to buy in Europe two first-class iron-clad cruisers at a cost of 1,400,000 pounds sterling. As the issue of the loan at 60 will produce 3,000,000 pounds sterling, there will remain 700,000 for the Ottoman treasury. The annuity to be paid is fixed at 173,000 pounds sterling, corresponding to the 87,000 pounds sterling required for the interest of the loan of consolidation, and to the 80,000 pounds sterling derived from the monopoly of the "*tumbeki*," granted two years since, and which was commencing to work.

It has been seen above that the imperial decree of December 20th gave to the holders of Ottoman bonds those portions of the Ottoman public debt referred, by virtue of the Treaty of Berlin, to Bulgaria, to Greece, and to Montenegro.

Notwithstanding the undeniable loyalty with which, even at the cost of great sacrifices, the government of the Sultan Abdul Hamid fulfilled the stipulation of the treaty, the execution of which was incumbent upon it, Europe tolerated that Bulgaria, Greece, Serbia, and Montenegro should disregard the pledges which they were bound to observe. There is in this evidently a want of firmness in the powers represented at the Congress of Berlin, as they should never have consented that their signatures should be protested by these petty states. A brief enumeration of the contributive shares, and the means, bearing the imprint of a benevolent equity, which the Imperial Ottoman Government had officially proposed for their regulation, will show at the same time both the importance for Turkey as well as for its creditors of a solution of this vexed question, and the moderation of which the government of the Sultan Abdul Hamid has given a remarkable proof.

According to the figures furnished by the administration of the Ottoman public debt, Bulgaria owed to the Imperial Ottoman treasury a nominal sum of 10,888,528 Turkish pounds, which, at one percent, represents an annual payment of 108,885 Turkish pounds. It is, then, this sum of 108,885 Turkish pounds that it would be necessary to capitalize. In taking four percent as the average rate of interest on state shares in Europe, Bulgaria would have no longer anything to pay as a contributive part of the Ottoman debt at the expiration of this period, the capital to be obtained having to represent an annuity at four percent, redeemable in one hundred years. Under these conditions, the sum necessary to replace an annuity of 108,885 Turkish pounds was 2,667,240 Turkish pounds. Admitting that Bulgaria could not procure this amount at a rate of interest less than six percent, redeemable in twenty-fire years, it would have to bear an annual outlay of 208,050 Turkish pounds. It found in this combination great advantages as well for the consolidation of its credit as for the realization of its important savings of the sum which it owed to the Ottoman Empire, advantages which should have brought about its cooperation to this project. In fact, if Bulgaria were (as it is bound to do) to model the annual payments of its share with the payments of the Ottoman public debt, the proportion thereof increasing with the progression of the revenues conceded, up to five percent, it would be compelled, in the event of this, to pay an annuity of 544,425 Turkish pounds. Moreover, it would never be able to settle beforehand the amount that it should pass to the credit of its treasury. If, to avoid the risk of a possibility of any uncertainty occurring during a whole century, one values very modestly at two per cent, the average annuity to be paid, Bulgaria would then have to pay for its share an annuity of 217,770 Turkish pounds, and this for one hundred years. The payment of an annual sum of 208,650 Turkish pounds during twenty-five years only was, then, a combination entirely to the advantage of the principality.

Treating the other states on the same footing as Bulgaria, the shares of Greece, Serbia, and Montenegro would stand as follows:

For Greece, an annuity of 28,459 Turkish pounds at four percent, redeemable in one hundred years, represented a capital of 574,373 Turkish pounds, the redemption of which in twenty-five years, at six percent interest, necessitated an annuity of 44,931 Turkish pounds.

For Serbia, an annuity of 23,182 Turkish pounds at the same rate of interest and terms of redemption gave a capital of 568,075 Turkish pounds, demanding, to be redeemed in twenty-five years, a sum of 34,084 Turkish pounds.

For Montenegro, an annuity of 1,088 Turkish pounds, on the same conditions, to wit, a capital of 26,659 Turkish pounds, the redemption of which in twenty-five years at six per cent, is worth 2,085 Turkish pounds.

If this combination, eminently practical, and which defies all criticism, had been adopted by the signing powers of the Treaty of Berlin, and imposed by them on these four states in question, Turkey would have entered into immediate possession of a sum of 3,830,347 Turkish pounds. By employing this sum in a manner as wise and reasonable as she has shown in the employment of her other capitals since the accession to the throne of the Sultan Abdul Hamid, Turkey could have reduced her national debt 19,000,000 Turkish pounds in a few years. The European creditors of the Ottoman Empire may then regret that their respective governments did not sustain the legal claims of the Imperial Ottoman Government based on equity; but they are obliged to bear a striking testimony to the integrity with which Turkey keeps her engagements, and to her ability to fulfill them in the best way for the interest of those with whom she has contracted them.

Up to this date the shares which composed the general debt of the Ottoman Empire were considered almost always as speculation securities. It would be well to examine into them and see if in the present moment this is the proper estimate of their standing.

During the first twenty years of its existence the Ottoman public debt, constantly enlarged by new issues, attracted a large number of patrons on account of the high interest which it offered to the public. The events of 1875 dispersed this clientele, and up to 1881 the stock exchanges of Europe were flooded with Ottoman shares. After the convention of December 20, 1881, reabsorption commenced which has continued without interruption during the last ten years. If the absorption is not yet completed, and if a considerable portion of the Ottoman debt remains still floating in the market, it is because the present position of the debt, as well as the radical transformation which it has sustained during these ten years in consequence of the reforms due to the initiative of the Sultan, are as yet only imperfectly understood by many people. However, if we base the ratio of the annual amount of the debt on the number of inhabitants and the number of square miles in the Ottoman Empire as compared with the other countries of Europe, a double fact is the outcome of this statistical study. In the first place, the Ottoman debt is relatively much less than the majority of other countries, considering their respective populations. In the second place, the area of territory of the Ottoman Empire being capable of bearing u population much more dense than that which today occupies it, the country may be considered to be, in a great measure, partially inhabited, so to speak; and as it is rich in the greatest natural resources, extraordinary results would accrue if these resources were turned to the best advantage. The traditional reputation of speculation securities is not, then, applicable to Ottoman securities.

The war indemnity has been regulated by the convention of May 14, 1882, signed between the Imperial Ottoman Government and the cabinet of St. Petersburg. Turkey redeemed its debt of 802,500,000 francs, or 35,000,000 Turkish pounds, by means of an annuity of 350,000 Turkish pounds, payable in one hundred years. In these figures are included the taxes on sheep and the tithes of the *vilayets* of Alep, Koniah, Castamouni, Adana, and Sivas; revenues which, in 1882, represented a total of 427,500 Turkish pounds. But, in consequence of famines which have sapped Asia Minor and Anterior Asia, as well as the poor crops which have prevailed for several years, these revenues have given returns less than were estimated as probable, which caused an increase of liabilities amounting, in 1888, to 600,000 Turkish pounds. A new agreement made between the two governments interested in the liquidation of these arrears gave to Russia the portions of the tithes of the vilayet of Alep which remained free, and the tithes of the *vilayet* of Mamouret-ul-Aziz. For six years the Russian Government was to put in its coffers an annuity of 450,000 Turkish pounds, instead of the original annuity of 350,000 Turkish pounds. As to the indemnity stipulated in favor of the Russian merchants residing in Turkey, and who had been commercially injured by the war of 1877-78, the commission *ad hoc* instituted for the investigation of claims amounting to 19,000,000 francs, had fixed the amount at 6,000,000 francs. In December, 1884, a first installment of 50,000 Turkish pounds was paid on account to the parties concerned.

The "Journal of the Chamber of Commerce of Constantinople" has published, under date of April 7, 1894, concerning the revenues ceded to the public Ottoman Debt, a very able article, of which the following is a translation:

"We reserve to ourselves to publish, as usual, in the near future, an analyzed report of the Council of

Administration, concerning the revenue ceded to the public Ottoman Debt, according to the proceedings of the year 1309 (1898-1894).

"Meanwhile we herewith set forth a few figures showing the general situation at the close of the year ending the 28th day of February, 1894, as compared to that of the year 1892-1893.

|  | 1893-94 | 1893-93 |
|---|---|---|
|  | TURKISH POUNDS | |
| Gross receipts from all sources | 2,543,735 | 2,508,760 |
| Expenses of the administration, and disbursements | 350,271 | 319,939 |
| Net receipts | 2,192,464 | 2,188,821 |
| Amount collected in the Central Bureau | 2,189,405 | 2,184,545 |
| Balance of redemption funds of the preceding year | 21,555 | 3,321 |
|  | 2,210,960 | 2,187,868 |
| To be deducted: |  |  |
| Balance according to new account | 108,715 | 104,826 |
| Reserve for the increase interest of debt | 2,102,245 | 2,083,040 |

To be added:
Interest on redeemed shares, net available amount for the service of the debt for the year

|  | 85,895 | 71,307 |
|---|---|---|
|  | 2,188,140 | 2,154,347 |

| To be deducted: | 1893-94 | 1892-93 |
|---|---|---|
| Service of priorities | 430,500 | 430,500 |
| Service of 1% interest on Series A, B, C, D, And bonds | 1,161,351 | 1,161,351 |
| Special service of loans 1863-64-65, and 1873 | 9,459 | 9,459 |
| | 1,601,310 | 1,601,310 |
| Balance available for redemption fund | 586,830 | 553,037 |

TURKISH POUNDS

| Ordinary Redemption Fund | 1893-94 | 1892-93 |
|---|---|---|
| Sum employed in repurchase of Series A (including interest of redeemed bonds) | 205,047 | 292,895 |
| Sum employed in repurchase of Series B (including interest of redeemed shares) | 99,206 | 74,329 |

Funds of Extraordinary Redemption accruing from Conversion of Priorities. Sums (including interest of redeemed bonds used for the redemption of Series A-D)

| | | |
|---|---|---|
| Series A | 11,738 | 11,554 |
| Series B | 55,751 | 54,027 |
| Series C | 58,274 | 55,538 |
| Series D | 45,448 | 43,139 |
| | 565,464 | 531,482 |

To be added:
Sum carried to redemption fund for future use

| | | |
|---|---|---|
| | 21,366 | 21,555 |
| Totals | 586,830 | 553,037 |

Nominal capital redeemed during the year:

|  | Ltg. | % | Ltg. | % |
|---|---|---|---|---|
| Series A | 489,000 | 57.03 | 516,000 | 53.64 |
| Series B | 404,000 | 34.87 | 380,000 | 30.70 |
| Series C | 223,080 | 23.75 | 234,000 | 21.58 |
| Series D | 185,200 | 22.31 | 186,000 | 21.08 |
|  | 1,301,280 | 39.50 | 1,316,000 | 36.71 |

## REDEMPTION FUND

| | TURKISH POUNDS | |
|---|---|---|
| | Original Nominal Capital | Redeemed Nominal Capital |
| 1$^{st}$ group, Series A | 7,119,882 | 5,270,110 |
| 2$^{nd}$ group, Series B | 10,044,825 | 1,234,500 |
| 3$^{rd}$ group, Series C | 30,549,251 | 842,080 |
| 4$^{th}$ group, Series D | 43,651,965 | 757,500 |
| 4$^{th}$ group, Turkish bonds 58% | | 281,000 |
| 4$^{th}$ group, Turkish bonds 20% | 14,211,407 | 110,741 |
| 4$^{th}$ group, Turkish bonds repurchase | | 332,548 |
| Totals | 105,577,330 | 8,828,479 |

Here follows the detailed account of receipts and expenses:

| | TURKISH POUNDS | |
|---|---|---|
| Receipts | 1893-94 | 1892-93 |
| Spirits, salt, stamps, fisheries, silks, and arrears in tobacco | 1,104,605 | 1,091,037 |
| Tithes on tobacco | 95,359 | 100,865 |
| Tobaccos (receipt of excise) | 750,000 | 750,000 |
| Part of the profits of excise | 37,084 | 21,745 |
| Tribute of Oriental Roumelia | 152,026 | 152,026 |

| | | | |
|---|---|---|---|
| Drafts on Customs Cyprus | | 102,596 | 102,590 |
| Drafts on Customs Tambeki | | 50,000 | 50,000 |
| | Totals | 2,291,670 | 2,268,269 |

TURKISH POUNDS

| Expenses | 1893-94 | 1892-93 |
|---|---|---|
| Expenses of the Central Board | 83,514 | 67,483 |
| Exchange loss on silver | 1,009 | 742 |
| Expenses and commissions | 16,188 | 17,735 |
| Totals | 100,711 | 85,960 |
| Profit of exchange on remittance | 7,861 | 2,878 |
| To be deducted, interest on deposit fund | 6,307 | 5,114 |
| Totals | 2,189,405 | 2,184,545 |

"As one may be convinced by the preceding tables, the general results of the proceedings of 1893-94 are more brilliant than those of any other years preceding.

"The special report of Mr. Vincent Caillard, on the subject of the Ottoman National Debt, for the year 1893-94 has also been published lately; as usual, it contains very interesting information as to the financial position of the Ottoman Empire.

"It appears out of the question, says Mr. Vincent Caillard, to hope that the conceded revenues could present each year an increase as important as that which was the object of my report of last year. The progress has in no way been as marked, but affairs seem likely to follow the same course.

"The gross revenues have risen to 2,542,735 Turkish pounds, against 2,508,760 Turkish pounds of the year preceding, showing an increase of 33,975 Turkish pounds, or 1.35 percent There has been, on the other hand, an increase of expenditures of 30,332 pounds, so that the net revenue only shows an increase of 3,643 Turkish pounds. If one compares the two years 1893-94, and 1891-92, the increase for the first is 110,631 Turkish pounds, or 5.28 percent.

"The increase of expenses has been due principally to the raising of salaries, and this measure was adopted to assure to the administration the services of more competent and experienced men. The number of inspector s has been increased, and the results obtained have been favorable. The effect produced by these reforms will, of course, be more perceptible at the end of the current year.

"Mr. Vincent Caillard also observes, on the other hand, that the collection of revenues has been made under considerable difficulties, in view of a very mediocre harvest and the universal fall in the price of cereals; but he thinks that the amount collected should be considered very satisfactory, and adds further on this point:

"The year 1894-95 will show better returns; one cannot be too well pleased in the matter; the fall in the price of grain having discouraged the farmers and reduced their resources, and this misfortune striking a population so essentially agricultural as that of Turkey. We must also bear in mind the quarantine enforced in Asia Minor in consequence of the cholera epidemic. Thus, in a year little favored by circumstances, it is already remarkable that the revenues have maintained their level, the conditions of the current year having been so far, not only not better but still worse than during the year 1893. But I think it would be vain to hope that the increase in receipts may continue, and if we do as well as last year we shall certainly have cause to be satisfied."

"Here is the passage of the report in which Mr. Vincent Caillard treats of the question of the reserve for increasing the interest on the debt:

"This reserve reaches at the end of 1893-94 the sum of 224,893 Turkish pounds, and it will in March, 1803, amount to 337,000. Now, to pay to the debt a quarter more per annum, it would require 292,700 Turkish pounds. The payment will then be possible, but it does not necessarily follow that it may be immediately effected. The Articles 10 and 11 of the decree of *Moukarrem* seem to say that the rate of interest should be legalized, hence the constitution of a reserve fund."

"The authors of the decree cannot have foreseen the fluctuation in rates of interest and the inextricable confusion which would result from it in the working of the redemption scheme. Their intention has been, probably, that the rates of interest once raised should remain so; and it is to give to the council the means of assuring this result that it has been given the power to constitute a reserve fund whence could be drawn, as occasion required, funds to fill slight deficits from one half year to the other."

"This, However, is the expression of the opinion of Mr. Vincent Caillard, and also as he remarks in his report (page 17) he maintained there is no doubt on the subject.

"Of all hazards," adds Mr. Vincent Caillard, "such appears to be the best policy in financial matters. At the same time I cannot deny that the letter of the decree gives a very plausible argument in favor of those who wish immediate payment of the one-fourth percent interest; the more so that the reserve has the necessary sum in hand, and without there being any need to consider if the rate of interest can or cannot be permanently maintained."

## THE ARMY

In its present organization, the work of the reign of the Sultan Abdul Hamid, the Ottoman army is divided into three great divisions, namely:

I. The *"Mouasaf"* (army of active service), composed of two subdivisions:

(1) The *"Nizam"* (army of active service, properly speaking), and

(2) The *"Ichtidî"* (army of active service on unlimited leave).

II. The *"Rédif"* (army of reserve), including also two subdivisions.

III. The *"Muntafiz"* (territorial army).

The total length of military service is fixed at twenty years: Active army, six years, of which four in the first subdivision and two in the latter. Army of reserve, eight years, four in each subdivision. Territorial army, six years. Only Muslims are admitted to military service. For non-Muslims the right of exacting military service is replaced by a tax — "*Bédél-i-askeriyeh.*" Every male Ottoman subject who is not a Muslim pays annually from birth this so-called blood-tax. This tax is collected by the respective communities and paid annually into the treasury. The law of organization of 1886, on army recruiting, has established obligatory service for every Mussulman in the empire, with the exception of the population of the capital, which is excepted in virtue of long-existing privileges. In the active army are not included: (1) the men-at-arms or mounted police of the capital and provinces; (2) the irregular troops; and (3) the contingent due by the Khedive of Egypt. The age of conscription is, since 1886, fixed at twenty-one, and the annual contingent is established on a footing of from 50,000 to 60,000 men. The non-called section being divided into two categories, the first, counting to rank, is required to submit to six and even nine months of military training annually, according to the importance of the localities in which is the residence of the men who compose it; the second only obliged to exercise once a week — Friday, after the noonday prayer.

In case of war, mobilization of the army would show:

(a) Active army (*nizam* and *ichtidt*), 350,000 men.

(b) Reserve army (*rédif*), 450,000 men.

(c) Territorial army (*muntafiz*), 200,000 men.

Thus, about a million of men, with 1,512 campaign pieces and 330 mountain pieces. All the military forces of the empire are distributed in army corps, placed under the command of a marshal or general of division. The staff of an army corps directs what concerns tactics; the council of the army corps, what concerns administration.

To the number of seven, the army corps have their headquarters in the following cities:

I. Constantinople, First Corps (Imperial Guard).

II. Adrianople, Second Corps.

III. Monastir, Third Corps.

IV. Erzinghiam, Fourth Corps.

V. Damascus, Fifth Corps.

VI. Bagdad, Sixth Corps.

VII. Yamen, Seventh Corps.

To these army corps one must add the military division of Tripoli, and the Hedjaz division.

The Ministry of War, or *"Serasker,"* is under the supreme orders of the Sultan, who is the chief of the army, which he directs and controls, with the assistance of the Grand Council of War, *"Dar-i-choura-i-askeriyeh,"* composed of one marshal and six generals of division, and of the council of the *"Grande Maîtrise"* of Artillery, *"Medjlis-i-tophaneh-amireh."* Appointed by the Sultan and depending directly from him as from the Ministry of War, the Grand Master of the Artillery has, by the very nature of his functions, which give him a high hand over the artillery and engineers, attributes of an importance almost equaling those of the Minister of War.

The Ottoman infantry has from all time been renowned for its power of resistance and impetuosity in attack. In an assault upon the enemy at the point of the bayonet, the Ottoman infantry is like a human avalanche, of which the tremendous impulse can be checked only by much superior force. In defending a place, a redoubt, the Turkish foot-soldier is always at his post, firm as a rock.

The equipment of the infantry is of the most simple and practical kind. Excepting for the battalions of the Imperial Guard, who wear the *Zouave* coat and trousers, the uniform is composed of a sort of coat of dark blue, trousers and leggings of same. The head-gear is a fez. Before long the infantry will be armed by Mauser repeating rifle — caliber, nine millimeters and a half — which the government of the Sultan decided in 1887 to substitute for the Martini-Henry rifles and the Remington rifles which had till then been used by Ottoman troops. A contract with Mauser & Co. to furnish to the Ottoman Government 500,000 repeating rifles for the infantry and 52,000 repeating rifles for the cavalry commenced to be put into execution in 1888, and the installment deliveries are nearly brought to a close.

The Turkish cavalry has a great advantage over European cavalries in so much as it can be more easily recruited from populations having from birth habits of horsemanship, whereas in Europe, where recruits have to be taken from everywhere, they come as frequently from the working classes and rural classes as from those who are habituated to riding. The service being of four instead of three years, as is the case in France and Germany, the Turkish cavalry derives from this longer service advantages which it is not necessary to point out to be thoroughly understood. If the modern strategical code has completely modified the conditions under which must now operate the actions of cavalry, it has in no way diminished the importance of it. With the repeating rifle and the far-reaching cannon the old-fashioned groupings on the battle-field and the great charges in a body can no longer be used. Cavalry is the eye of an army as well as the veil behind which it conceals its movements. A numerous cavalry is thus indispensable to a proper military organization. The Turkish cavalry numbers thirty-five regiments of five squadrons. This number might seem little in keeping with the military condition of Turkey, but the Sultan has found in the patriotism of his faithful subjects a method of doubling — and even more than that — his cavalry forces in time of war. The armament of Ottoman cavalry is composed of slightly curved swords and small-caliber rifles. A certain number of regiments are furnished with a lance, and everything tends to the supposition that these will be distributed to the rest of the cavalry. The uniform consists of a simple tunic with one row of buttons, a pair of gray trousers, and Prussian boots. The horses belong generally to the Turco-Persian breed or Arab cross-breed. Of rather small build, of delicate form, nervous, with supple legs, and indefatigable, these horses are both very intelligent and very docile.

The campaign artillery comprises 252 batteries of six pieces, besides 56 mountain batteries also of six pieces. All the artillery, of fortress or campaign, including guns and accessories, come from the Krupp factories at Essen; but there are also constructed cannons upon these models at the great artillery works at Tophané (Constantinople). The mountain batteries deserve really special mention, on account of the exceptional dexterity of their maneuvers. The cannon, frame, and ammunition are carried by four mules; to unload them and put the cannon in readiness takes not two minutes. The uniform of the artillery consists of a dark blue dolman, with black frogs, a pair of gray trousers, and boots. Instead of the fez of the infantry, the cavalry and artillery wear a black hair *kalpak*, similar to that which was worn prior to 1870 by the *"chasseurs à cheval"* and the French *hussars*. The officer corps is recruited among the under officers and the students of the military schools of Coumbar-bané and Pancaldi — the first for the artillery, the second for the infantry, the cavalry, and the staff.

Until the last war, the general staff did not exist in Turkey, and one can really attribute to its absence a great influence on the issue of the campaign. Thanks to the Sultan Abdul Hamid, this deficiency is filled. The school of Pancaldi possesses, since 1884, a section of staff which corresponds to the German War Academy and the Superior War College of France.

At the Artillery and Engineering School students enter at the age of fifteen years, spend four years in the preparatory division, two years in the superior division, and are then promoted to the rank of under-lieutenant, and, after another year of finishing studies, issue forth with the rank of lieutenant.

At the school of Pancaldi the students pass three years, and issue forth with the rank of under-lieutenant. The best students, who are destined to the staff corps, remain another three years, and then issue forth with the rank of captain.

The organization of these two great schools leaves nothing to be desired regarding discipline and theoretic and practical instruction. The study of foreign languages is notably more developed than in the military schools of other countries.

Under the Coumbar-hané and Pancaldi schools are preparatory schools (*"Mekteb-i-Idadié-Harbieh"*), at Adrianople, Monastir, Broussa, Erzeroum, Damascus, and Bagdad, at Koubeli, and in the suburbs of Constantinople, on the Asiatic side of the Bosphorus. This last is directed by a brigadier-general, the others being commanded by lieutenant-colonels or chiefs of battalion. Pupils enter at the age of twelve, and spend there three years.

## THE NAVY

Notwithstanding that the Ottoman navy played a most honorable role in the war of 1877-78, the issue of the war left it somewhat disorganized. The navy, no less than the army, required a reorganization. This reorganization, pursued by the Sultan with that foresight and tenacity which he brings to bear upon the execution of all his reformatory plans, is now accomplished. It remains only to put the finishing touches on the details of the putting into practice — secondary points, accessory to the principal lines. The Ottoman navy today comprises, according to the last official statistics of 1894, the following ships:

*Iron-clads* — Seven frigates, three imperial yachts, three pontoons, and twenty-one torpedo-boats — this actual number nearly doubled; two submarine boats of the Nordenfeldt system, measuring in all 69,697 tons, with 39,946 nominal horsepower, and carrying 360 Krupp, Armstrong, and Nordenfeldt guns. They are manned by 5,420 men and 505 officers.

*Wooden Vessels, Steamers* — Three frigates, seven corvettes and twelve armed coast-guards, eighteen schooners — in all, forty ships, measuring 40,912 tons, with 1,913 nominal horsepower, carrying 318 guns of different calibers. They are manned by 7,454 men and 695 officers.

*Sailing Vessels* — One training ship, one schooner, one aviso, thirty transports — in all, of 8,275 tons.

Among the iron-clad frigates one must mention the *Hamidié*, launched in 1885 from the dockyards of the Admiralty at Constantinople, a superb ship, which proves that the Turks, in point of naval construction, can rival other maritime powers.

At this moment a number of frigates and corvettes are being repaired and overhauled at the dockyards of Constantinople and Ismit, to render them suitable to modern naval tactics.

The government of the Sultan has chosen for the defense of the coast of the empire and the armament of its iron-clads, the torpedoes, on account of their simple construction as well as their efficacy. An alien fleet endeavoring to force itself through the Dardanelles would inevitably meet with disastrous losses. Between the fires of the fortresses on both the European and Asiatic coasts, and exposed every minute to being blown up by torpedoes, of which a succession of rows bar the passage, alien vessels could never reach the point of Nagara. If some should, however, succeed by the action of the current in passing this first defense, they would inevitably come into contact with the Ottoman men-of-war, which would, assisted by the forts which line the coast, make short work of the already partly disabled vessels. Besides which, it is only he who is master of the European coast who is master of the Dardanelles, the coast of Asia being of lesser importance, and all attempt at disembarkation, whether on the Gallipolean peninsula or more to the west, would lead to a signal defeat of the assailant, whose troops, crushed by the superior forces of the Ottoman army of observation, would be unable even to seek refuge in their ships, and would undoubtedly be compelled to surrender their arms.

The length of service in the navy is twelve years; five in active service (*nizam*), three in the reserve of the active service (*ichtidt*), and four in the reserve proper (*rédif*).

The officer corps, furnished by the naval school of Halki, envies nothing in the officers of either the French or English navies.

The Sultan has desired to give to the merchant marine all the encouragement necessary to its proper development. It is to its present sovereign that Turkey owes its commercial naval school, founded at Halki some four years since, and which trains the captains of the great and little coasting traders, as well as the captains of the ships for more distant traffic, who will render signal service in naval mobilization.

From the Ministry of the Navy depend also a regiment of infantry of marine of 5,000 or 6,000 men, which deserves mention here as among the most splendid troops of the empire.

From the point of view of naval organization Turkey is divided into nine naval stations: Constantinople, Scutari, Chio, Preveza, Salonica, Crete, Tripoli (Africa), Bassorah and the Persian Gulf, Jeddah and the Red Sea. After the disasters of 1870-71, France took twenty years to reconstitute its military condition. Turkey has succeeded in the same task in half the time. It is the most powerful eulogy which one can make to the Ottoman Empire and its able sovereign.

## PUBLIC INSTRUCTION AND SCHOOLS

Formerly instruction of Muslims in Turkey was entirely concentrated in the mosque. The *médressés* of Constantinople enjoyed a universal reputation, for, according to the celebrated maxim, "the study of science was a precept divine for the true believers." Two kinds of schools then existed: the *mektebs*, or elementary schools, entrusted to the *imams*, or religious men of the various quarters; and the *médressés*, or schools of theology, of jurisprudence, and of philosophy annexed to the great mosques. All were supported by the *Vakoufs* administration. There were no middle schools. Thus students left the primary schools without sufficient preparation to enter profitably into the more advanced studies. The secularization of public instruction substituted state instruction is the schools for that of the mosque, excepting in the case of the *médressés*, which remained always in the sphere of the attributes of the *Sheikh-ul-Islamat*. Such transformations cannot be accomplished at once; a period of trials is always necessary to practically realize the reforms decreed on paper. Without a good system of practical application, theory, even though of the highest order, is condemned to unproductiveness. It was this method of practical application which was lacking, and no amount of firmness or zeal displayed by the Ottoman Government could obtain the results due to such efforts.

Before 1876, with the exception of some few establishments of superior instruction maintained by the government at Constantinople, public instruction — that is, as far as the Muslim population was concerned — was reduced to the most slender proportions. Organized in a most primitive manner, the primary schools could give to the youth of the Muslim population who came to them for instruction only an education of the most rudimentary character, and at best most imperfect and incomplete. One learned there barely to read and write, particularly in the provinces, where geography and history were generally the objects of no solicitude. Secondary instruction and superior instruction did not present themselves at all under a favorable aspect. No doubt at Constantinople young men of the more distinguished classes had the opportunities of causing themselves to be admitted to the special governmental schools, or to foreign colleges, but in the primary schools resources of this nature did not exist.

Today the situation is completely changed. Public instruction shines in Turkey; its light has dispelled the darkness and illumines even the most distant regions of the empire. Convinced that to spread knowledge is to augment his power, the Sultan Abdul Hamid puts into practice the precept of the Prophet, *"Look for knowledge, even though it be in China,"* and causes the Ottoman Empire to take a first rank in intellectual culture. The organizing law concerning public instruction divides, theoretically, the schools of the empire into two categories — public schools, of which the administration belongs exclusively to the state; and private schools, placed only under the supervision of the government, they being founded and carried on directly by individuals or communities. To this last category belong the *médressés* and the non-Muslim schools. The instruction of the public schools comprises three grades — primary, secondary, superior.

## PRIMARY INSTRUCTION

This includes three kinds of schools — the *mukiatibi sibian*, which one can compare to the children's asylums of Central Europe; the *ibdadiés*, or primary schools proper, and the *ruschdiyehs*, or superior primary schools. In the *ibdadiés* the course is four years, and the curriculum includes the following studies: Primary spelling (Turkish), verses or stanzas of the Qur'an, reading in Turkish, calligraphy, Turkish grammar, arithmetic, geography, history. (For Muslims, primary instruction is gratuitous and obligatory. All fathers of families are obliged by law to present themselves before the head of the municipality of the quarter in which they reside — *mouktar* — for the purpose of causing to be inscribed their children of both sexes, at the age of six, on the registers of the *sibians* or *ibdadiés*, unless they prove their means of giving at home the proper primary education to their children.

The *ruschdiyeh* schools receive children at the age of ten or twelve years, who there spend four years. There the programme of studies is as follows: Grammar and syntax, Turkish, Arab, and Persian; orthography, composition, and style; history of the Ottoman Empire and universal history; geography, arithmetic, elements of geometry, linear drawing, and the language of one of the non-Muslim communities of the locality.

For girls, the instruction comprehends religious instruction, Turkish grammar, elements of Arab and Persian grammars, a few hints as to literature, history, and geography; arithmetic, domestic economy, needlework, drawing and music; the last elective.

Each community of five hundred Muslim houses must have a *ruschdiyeh* school.

The higher primary instruction is also gratuitous, without being obligatory.

All expenses, maintenance of schools, salary of professors, purchases of books and instruments of work for students, are made at the cost of the treasury.

The last statistics, published some years since, show that primary schools in the capital were:

*Sibian* schools, 263; of which 142 for boys and 123 for girls; attended by 6,909 children of the masculine sex, and 4,734 of the feminine sex.

*Ibdadié* schools, 40; of which 32 for boys and 8 for girls; attended by 1,601 boys and 93 girls.

*Ruschdiyeh* schools, 29; of which 19 for boys and 10 for girls; attended by 1,180 boys and 353 girls.

In the provinces each village, no matter how small, possesses a *sibian* school, and villages of some importance an *ibdadié* school.

Primary schools are more frequented each year, and one can safely say that, under the reign of the present Sultan, of every 100 children, 98 at least receive a good primary education.

The *ruschdiyeh* schools in the provinces number 371, of which three are for girls — two at Beyrout and one at Broussa — and are attended by 14,914 children. Today the number has perceptibly increased.

## SECONDARY INSTRUCTION

This includes two kinds of schools, the *ibdadiés*, or preparatory schools, and the *sultaniés*, or colleges.

The *ibdadié* schools are mixed and receive all children, whether Muslim or non-Muslim, who have followed all the classes of the *ruschdiyeh* schools and have passed the coming-out examination. Every city of 1,000 houses has an *ibdadié* school. The length of course is three years, and the studies comprise Ottoman literature, epistolary style, French, rhetoric, elements of political economy, geography, universal history, arithmetic, algebra, geometry, land surveying, physics, chemistry, natural history, and drawing. The colleges must be established at the capital or chief town of each *vilayet*. They are separated into two divisions — one a grammar school, in which the studies pursued are similar to those pursued in the *ibdadié* schools; and another more advanced department, itself redivided into sections, that of letters and that of science. In each one of the divisions the length of the course is fixed at three years. These colleges, which will be opened one after another, as soon, as the budget will warrant the necessary expenditure consequent upon their proper maintenance, have as a prototype the Imperial College of Galata Seraï ("*Mekteb Sultani*") at Péra, which was organized after the models of the great establishments of secondary instruction in France. The corps of professors is partly composed of Europeans, and the instruction is given in the French language. The direction and administration of these colleges, however, is Ottoman. The length of the course is five years, not including the three years of preparatory studies for those children who do not, at the time of their admission to the college, possess sufficient of the knowledge which is the object of the primary instruction.

According to the last regulations decided upon by the government of the Sultan, the curriculum of studies includes : the Turkish language, the Arabian language, the French language; Turkish and French calligraphy, Turkish and French literature, and the translation of the Turkish into French, and of the French into Turkish; philosophy, Ottoman history of Islam, elements of the Latin tongue necessary to the study of pharmacy, medicine, and law; geography, political, administrative, commercial, agricultural, and industrial, of the principal states, and more particularly of the Ottoman Empire; mathematics, bookkeeping, linear drawing; the Greek, Armenian, German, English, and Italian languages — these electively.

The University (or college) of Galata Seraï gives diplomas of bachelor (*bachelier*), which rank with those given by the state in France.

Included in the category of institutions for secondary instruction are also:

(1) The Imperial Civil School of "*Mekteb-Mulkié-Chahané*," at Stamboul, placed under the august patronage of the Sultan Abdul Hamid, who founded it and maintains it entirely at his expense. There are taught canon law (*fetwa-i-cherif*), commercial law, civil legislation, general history, political economy, editorship, bookkeeping, geography, French, natural history, chemistry. Students, who have successfully passed the final examinations and graduated, have right to the position of *Caïmakam* in the provincial administration, or to the functions of an equal grade in the various departments of the state.

(2) The International Ottoman School for young girls, founded in 1880 at Stamboul by the Sultan Abdul Hamid, who has always manifested the most signal solicitude for the education of girls. The studies include the following: Turkish language, Armenian and Greek; French, German, English, and Russian—the last four elective; geography, natural history, piano, vocal music, and needlework.

In virtue of the law of organization of 1884, concerning instruction, there exists in each vilayet a direction and inspection bureau of public instruction.

# SUPERIOR INSTRUCTION

In Europe universities possess five departments, with a respective faculty each, namely: letters, science, law, medicine, theology. In the Ottoman university there could be no question of a medical faculty and department, as there existed already a School of Medicine, fulfilling all the requirements of that branch of study, and which had a separate general management depending upon the Ministry of War. As regarded a theological faculty and department, great difficulties existed. It would have been necessary to appoint as many theological faculties as there exist sects in the empire. There could be no question of this; besides which such chairs would have been entirely superfluous, as each one of these sects provided independently, according to its lights, its own theological instruction, having therein the greatest freedom possible. There remained, therefore, the faculties and departments of law, letters, and science, which are represented, the first by the School of Law; the second by the School of Letters and Philology; the third by the School of Engineering.

(1) The School of Law ("*Houkouk Mektebi*") was founded on the coming to the throne of the Sultan Abdul Hamid, by the transforming into public chairs those of elementary law and political economy belonging to the Galata Seraï College. In 1882 the School of Law was entirely reorganized upon a permanent basis. The length of the course is four years, and the studies include Ottoman law ("*Medjellé*"), Mussulman law, Roman or civil law, Roman institutions from the historical point of view, commercial Ottoman law, civil and commercial procedure, penal and criminal law, administrative law, and political economy.

(2) The School of Letters and Philology ("*Edebuyat-i-aliyeh Mektebi*") comprises the following courses: Arab literature, Greek literature, Latin literature, logic, philosophy, archaeology, universal history, and the philosophy of history.

(3) The School of Engineering ("*Tourouk-i-meabir Mektebi*"), formerly annexed to the Galata Seraï College under the name of "School of Civil Engineering" ("*Mulkié Mehendiz Mektebi*"), was finally separated therefrom in the first year of the reign of the Sultan Abdul Hamid, and became what it is now. The course is four years, as in the other departments.

61

Among the special schools, one must distinguish those which, placed among the dependencies of the Ministry of Public Instruction, constitute, with the university itself, the superior instruction of the state; and the special schools, properly speaking, depending on the different ministries.

The first are six in number:

(1) The Civil School of Medicine (*"Mektebi Tebiei Mulkié"*), at Stamboul, separated since 1882 from the Imperial School of Medicine, and placed under the Ministry of Public Instruction. The students who leave this school with their degree of doctor have right to the grade of *salissé* and a position as municipal physician.

If the *Séraskérat* or the Admiralty require to engage other supplementary physicians, they have to give the preference to the students of this school.

(2), (3), and (4) three Normal Schools, namely: *"Dar-ul-Moualemi-i-Sebian,"* to form the teachers of the elementary primary schools; *"Dar-ul-Moualemi-i-Ruschdiyeh,"* which turns out the professors of the superior primary schools; *"Dar-ul-Moualémal,"* which is specially for the young girls destined to professorships.

(5) The School of Languages, established by an imperial irade of the Sultan Abdul Hamid in the month of October, 1883, for the officials or employees of the Sublime Porte and of the Ministry of Foreign Affairs, not having passed the age of twenty-five years. The course of five years includes grammar, editorship in French, translation from Turkish to French and *vice versa*, the Turkish, Arabian, and French languages — these obligatory; Greek, Armenian, English, German, and Russian, elective.

Not only employees of the departments of State and Public Administration have the right of following these courses, but foreign students can cause themselves to be admitted on payment of twenty-five Turkish pounds per annum. The degrees conferred by this school give right to employment under the government in the various departments and in the bureaus of translation.

(6) The School of Fine Arts, founded by the present Sultan in 1883, and installed at Gul-hané (Stamboul), by the side of the Imperial Ottoman Museum and annexed to its administration, includes departments of painting, sculpture, engraving, architecture. Its administration is a prototype, in theory at least, of the *"École des Beaux Arts"* at Paris.

Formerly the Ottoman Empire had spread a brilliant glow by its art; but if in letters and science it had always been able to oppose to those of the Occident names equally illustrious, this had not been recently the case with regard to the fine arts. Architecture, sculpture, painting had fallen into a profound decadence. The architects to whom we owe the erection of the magnificent mosques of Suleymania, of the Sultan Ahmed, of Jeni Djami, etc., which contest for the palm with the most stately monuments of Europe; the sculptors whose chisels had created arabesques which are as though laces of stone; the artists who had painted those porcelains and decorated those ceilings which are the admiration of strangers, no longer lived in their successors. From the day on which the Sultan Abdul Hamid ascended the throne of Osman, Turkey began to shake itself from the artistic torpor into which it had fallen. Formerly all the antiquities discovered on Ottoman soil passed into foreign countries and went to ornament the museums of Europe. It is thus that the magnificent *"Gigantomachia"* adorns the Museum of Berlin, and the antiquities of Nineveh are in the museums of London and Paris. Today the Imperial Ottoman Government is no longer robbed of its legitimate possessions, and the Museum of Constantinople, become worthy of its name, excites the admiration of visitors, as it possesses treasures like the tomb of Alexander the Great, discovered five years ago at Saïda, and which defy all comparisons.

Among the schools of superior instruction which today bear witness in Turkey to the enlightened interest which the Sultan takes in the study of *"belles-lettres,"* and of the care unending with which he endeavors to widen the knowledge of the servants of the state, one must name the "School of High Diplomatic Studies," destined to rival the School of Political Science of Paris.

Those schools depending on other ministries than that of Public Instruction are—

(1) Depending on the Ministry of Commerce, of Public Works, and Agriculture:

(a) The Commercial School (*"Hamidié"*), founded in 1882 by the Sultan Abdul Hamid, who has provided the Ottoman Empire with an institution most useful to the development of industry and commerce.

(b) The schools of arts and trades (*"Mekteb Sanaï"*), two in number, one for boys and one for girls. This latter, which was entirely reorganized in 1883, can be cited as a model of its kind. There one learns reading, writing, and needlework. The work produced by the young girls is sold to their advantage, and the sums thus obtained are placed in a sort of savings-bank, to be distributed to the graduates according to merit.

(c) The professional schools, the founding and establishing of which was decided in 1884, one to each *vilayet*, and of which the establishing is progressing methodically.

(2) Schools depending on the Ministry of Finance:

(a) The School of Mines and Forestry, formed by the fusion, in the reign of the Sultan Abdul Hamid, of the School of Mines and of the School of Forestry.

(b) The School of Telegraphy, which owes to the enlightened patronage of the Sultan the importance which it has acquired.

Before passing in review the schools of the non-Muslims communities of the empire, it is necessary to devote a few lines to the instruction in the "*médressés*." In the *médressés* the studies are divided into ten branches, namely: grammar, syntax, logic, metaphysics, philology, figures of speech, style, rhetoric, geometry, astronomy. After ten or twelve years of study in the *médressés*, students are free to become *kadis* or of *mufti* or of imam. Those who desire to arrive at the very highest positions of the law must devote a certain number of additional years to the study of dogma, law, commentaries of the written law, and oral traditions. Besides the *médressés*, and also depending on the *Sheikh-ul-Islamat*, are the school for orphans of the "*Magiobats-du-cheri*" and the two schools of Stamboul and Scutari for the "*imams*" and the "*muezzins*"; founded, all three, in 1883, by the Sultan Abdul Hamid. Constantinople possesses a great number of public libraries (over forty), which are generally established in mosques, of which they form dependencies. They are open to the public every day in the week, Tuesdays and Fridays excepted. Besides the public libraries, the capital possesses over a thousand private libraries, the outcome of pious legacies made to mosques.

The schools of non-Muslim communities of the empire enter the category of establishments of public instruction designated by law free establishments. Once the permission obtained from the imperial authorities to open them, these establishments are managed in total independence of the state, which reserves to itself only the right to see that the instruction contains nothing contrary to the institutions of the empire or to morality, and that the professors belonging to these establishments possess the required degrees given by the Minister of Public Instruction, by the academic council of the *vilayet* in which they are situated, or by the ecclesiastical authorities of the community itself. Apart from these restrictions, necessary to maintain the rights of the state, the non-Muslim schools are free from all government interference. It is, indeed, a beautiful example of toleration which the Imperial Ottoman Government gives to other nations, and of which none can but realize the elevated character. Of all the schools of non-Muslim communities, those of the Greek Orthodox community are the most important, both on account of their number and of the high grade and efficiency of the studies. They are divided into three categories: parochial schools, private schools, and central superior schools. The first, founded and maintained by the parishes, comprehend the primary mutual schools, the Hellenic schools, and the girls schools. They correspond to the sibians, the *ibdadiés*, and the ruschdiyehs. The second, corresponding to the *ibdadiés*, are the establishments of secondary instruction founded by individuals. The third can be compared to the superior schools of the state. Among these latter one distinguishes particularly the "Great National School" of Phanar, the commercial and theological school of Halki. The library of the Great National School comprises nearly twenty thousand volumes.

To the number of over a hundred at Constantinople and its suburbs, the Greek schools are attended by some eleven to twelve thousand students, of whom three-quarters are of the masculine sex.

One of the communities, which has profited the most by the innumerable encouragements given to education and public instruction by the Sultan Abdul Hamid, is the Armenian community. Armenians, therefore, ought to be grateful and thankful to the Sultan. Before this reign, the Armenian community possessed but a most restricted number of schools in the capital and a few large cities. At Constantinople each parish had a primary school, where the instruction was limited to reading, writing, elementary arithmetic, catechism, and church singing for those children who possessed good voices. In some of these schools there were taught, besides, grammar, history, geography, and a little mathematics. Under the influence of the civilizing thought of the Sultan, the Armenian community has realized the most rapid progress in public instruction, and its schools rank now with the other educational establishments of the empire. It is particularly in the capital that the intellectual movement among the

Armenians has become the more pronounced. There are about 200,000 of them distributed through the city, but they are particularly grouped in 36 quarters and suburbs, where they possess 39 churches, on which depend 51 primary schools for boys and girls. In the greater number of the schools the instruction is gratuitous, it being the community which maintains them at its expense. They are attended by about 6,000 children, of whom 4,000 are boys and 2,000 girls.

Among the schools of the secondary class one must name the Berberian school, the Aigha-Zian school, the Mesbourian school for girls at Scutari, the Meschdoudjian school at Yeni Capoa, and the Teridyanian school at Coum Capoa. All these secondary schools have been founded by private individuals. The Armenian hospital at Yedi-coulé possesses a professional school for orphans of both sexes. It has 425 students, of whom 206 are boys and 219 girls. At Haskeny is an asylum for abandoned orphans, directed by the Armenian sisters. Among all the Armenian schools, one distinguishes in the first rank the "Central School" of Galata, where 150 students of the male sex receive secondary instruction. The faculty is composed of Armenian, Turkish, and European professors, taken from the faculty of the Imperial College at Galata-Seraï. The programme of studies includes religion, Armenian language and literature, Turkish language, French and German, calligraphy, drawing, geography, general history, philosophy, natural history, physics, chemistry, mathematics, law, political economy, bookkeeping, pedagogy, hygiene, and gymnastics. Founded in 1886, this school has already produced excellent results. It does honor as well to those who direct it as to the faculty.

In order to cause the co-religionists to participate also in the benefits and advantages of public instruction, the Armenians have founded, for the propagation of learning, divers societies, such as the Parikordzagan, Asiagan, Vartanian, Sinékérimian, etc. The most meritorious of all is unquestionably the "United Armenian Societies," created under the reign of Abdul Hamid. The sovereign himself grants to it annually large subsidies, in order better to enable this association to develop the educational system among his faithful subjects of Asiatic Turkey. This society maintains thirty-five schools for boys, attended by 2,362 pupils, and ten schools for girls, attended by 839 pupils. Thanks to it, 3,201 poor children receive gratuitous primary instruction.

Two societies of ladies, founded equally under the reign of Abdul Hamid, *vie* with the men's societies for the instruction of poor children of the feminine sex in the provinces. These are:

(1) The *"Tebrotzacer Hahyouhiatz"* Society, which turns out female teachers for the girls' schools in the provinces. It possesses a normal school at Stamboul, numbering eighty students. Since its organization this school furnishes some thirty female teachers annually to the different schools in the provinces.

(2) The *"Askananer Hahyouhiatz"* Society, which has as its aim the founding of girls' schools in those districts where they do not exist, and maintaining them. It has established up to now five primary schools, attended by 500 students.

In the capital, young girls receive superior instruction at the professional school at Péra. It counts 150 students, as well in the preparatory as in the superior department. In order to be therein admitted it is necessary to have previously had primary instruction. Outside the studies properly speaking, the programme includes needlework of every kind, which work is executed under the supervision of instructresses specially engaged in foreign countries. The students of superior classes have, indeed, made *trousseaux* for marriages, and Oriental embroideries of rare perfection.

It is necessary to mention here the *"Sanassarian"* school of Erzeroum, which owes its foundation, in 1881, to an Armenian Russian, native of Van, with the authorization of the Sultan Abdul Hamid. This school, by which profit particularly the *vilayets* of Anterior Asia, gives a secondary instruction. The faculty is composed of professors taken from German universities. One learns there also several manual trades, such as those of shoemaker, joiner, blacksmith, etc. Agriculture and horticulture are also taught by specialists from the Orient and from Europe.

Though not numerous — as the members of that community are very restricted in number — the schools of the Armenian Catholics are directed with care. Those of the Melchites of Venice and Vienna, the school of the patriarchate, and the Hamazkiatz, deserve special mention. A school directed by nuns gives primary instruction to the feminine sex.

After the Greek and Armenian schools come the Israelite schools, all founded and maintained by several rich individuals, or by the Universal Israelite Alliance. At the commencement of 1890 there existed in the entire Ottoman Empire seventeen of these schools for boys, frequented by 2,935 students; and thirteen schools for girls, frequented by 2,309 students; besides one mixed school — boys and girls — with 101 students. The programme of these schools is about the same as that of the *ruschdiyehs*. It includes the Hebrew tongue, Jewish history, modern history, geography, arithmetic, bookkeeping, elementary geometry, elementary notions of physics, of chemistry, natural history, and, as required by the various localities, the Turkish, Arabian, Greek, Italian, and Spanish languages. Superior instruction does not exist in the Israelite community; on the other hand, this community possesses ten professional schools for boys, and nine for girls, attended, the former by 240 apprentices, and the latter by 215 apprentices.

The wide hospitality which the Ottoman Empire affords to strangers is not lacking in the establishments of public instruction founded by Europeans, both in the capital and in the provinces. All requests for authorization to open schools presented by foreigners have always met with the best reception by the government of Abdul Hamid. It is thus that one sees in all parts of the Ottoman Empire French, Italian, English, Austrian, German, and American schools, prospering under the tutelary shield of the sovereign, in whom letters, science, and the arts have found the most powerful and magnanimous patron. At Constantinople alone one counts twenty-five schools, orphan asylums, and colleges, directed by Lazarists, Brothers of the Christian Schools, Sisters of Charity, and other Catholic religious orders, in which instruction is given to over 2,500 students of both sexes. There are, besides, five Protestant schools directed by English and American missions, one Helleno-Catholic school, and a dozen secular establishments of public instruction (which are either – superior, primary, or secondary).

A rich American has founded Robert College, remarkable for its superior instruction. The American Mission possesses besides a school, highly thought of, for the education of young girls.

At Beyrout is a free school of medicine, of which the usefulness in Arab-speaking countries is of inestimable value.

At Adrianople, Salonica, Janina, Smyrna, Trebizond, Aïntab, Mossul, etc., are also foreign schools, which aid the Ottoman schools in the progress of public instruction.

Every year the Sultan devotes to the advancement of public instruction considerable sums from his privy purse. Not only does the Padishah give the money necessary to the construction and maintenance of *sibian* and *ibdadiés* schools for boys and girls in those localities where the required funds are lacking, but he is constantly assisting the schools, either by pecuniary aid, which he grants to them with the liberality which belongs only to great kings, or by gifts of every nature, and prizes destined for the students, in order the better to stimulate their zeal. These good works the Sultan distributes among all his subjects, without distinction as to religion. As we have already said, all his subjects, sons of the same country, are absolutely equal. Indeed, every year, when his Majesty goes in state to Stamboul to the ceremony of "*Hirkai-cherif,*" he is greeted with enthusiasm by the students and professors of non-Muslim schools, placed in line along the streets of the city through which he passes. And the cries of "*Padischahim tchok yacha!*" are but a feeble demonstration of the unlimited gratitude which the people feel for their sovereign.

## THE ARMENIANS

Before closing the description of the remarkable progress made in Turkey under the reigning Sultan, we think it useful to say also a few words on the Armenian agitation we have been witnessing for the last three months, as well as on the legal status of the Armenians naturalized in the United States on their return to Turkey.

According to a well-known proverb in Turkey, it requires six Jews to deceive one Armenian. This proverb shows in what estimation Armenians in general are held in the East as to their truthfulness and honesty. The Armenians themselves seem to be well aware of their deficiency in this respect, for not long ago one of them had published in a leading newspaper of New York a letter to urge his co-religionists to be careful to tell in their statements the truth, only the truth, and nothing but the truth. How this simple-minded Armenian was successful in his endeavors and recommendations may be surmised by the following incident which has received a wide publicity throughout the United States and Europe:

"The story which has been thrilling: the world for some time past of the wife of the Armenian leader, Grego, who, rather than suffer dishonor at the hands of her Turkish persecutors, threw herself, with her child in her arms, into an abyss, and was followed by other women until the ravine was filled with corpses, has been exploded, as many persons predicted it would be, at the time it was sprung upon the public.

"It has been discovered that the horrible narrative is a reproduction, with additions and embellishments to suit the occasion, of an old tale told in poetry by Mrs. Hemans years ago, under the title of 'The Suliote Mother.' This discovery suggests the possibility, not to say probability, that the "Armenian atrocities" were to a large extent figments of the brain of some imaginative fanatic, originated for gain, revenge, or with some other similar object, and has caused a marked cessation of the anti-Turkish excitement upon all sides, except among the professional Armenian agitators, who have always been addicted to paroxysms of activity.

"These persons refuse to believe the story to have no better foundation than the rhyme, and await in perfect confidence the report of the investigating commission, which is already in Armenian territory."

Evidently there have been troubles at Sassoun, which will be investigated, the firm wishes of the Sultan being to treat all his subjects with justice, and to punish, according to law, all guilty parties. But it is, we think, interesting to know, first, what actually happened out there; and, second, who were the real aggressors.

Facts may be summed up in the following concise manner, as published by the *New York Herald*:

"The Armenian agitators that made their appearance in the steep mountains of Talouri, situated between Sassoun, in the southeast of Moush (*vilayet* of Bitlis), and the district of Call, of the Mutessarufat of Guendj, combined their forces together at the instigation of a certain Hampartzoum, who, under the assumed name of Mourat, was already giving trouble in those regions. This Hampartzoum, born in Hadjin (*vilayet* of Adana), after having for eight years studied medicine in the Civil Medical School of Constantinople, and participated in the disorders of Coum Capou, fled to Athens, and thence to Genoa. He afterwards went disguised, and again under an assumed name, by way of Alexandrette, from Diarbekir to the neighborhood of Bitlis, and he began then and there his seditious agitation, together with five other individuals.

"Hampartzoum was giving positive assurances to credulous people that he was a foreign agent, backed by all the European powers in his plans to upset the Turkish authorities. He succeeded thus in gaining to his criminal ends the Armenians of the villages of Siner, Simai, Gulli-Guzat, Ahi, Hedenk, Sinank, Chekind, Elffard, Moussone, Etek, Akdjesser, as well as those of the small borough of Talouri, comprising four districts.

"Now, these insurgents, under the command of Hampartzoum, abandoning, toward the latter part of July last, their respective villages, and after having placed in inaccessible spots their wives, children, and belongings, and secured also the cooperation of other armed insurgents that came from the Valley of Moush, and from the cazas of Call and Selvan, assembled together, numbering more than three thousand, at a place called Endouk-Dagh. Five or six hundred of them decided to fall upon Moush. They began by attacking the tribe of Delikan, on the Mount Courlink, in the south of Moush, killed a few of them, and robbed them of their belongings. All Muslims that fell into their hands were insulted in their religion, and murdered in a most horrible manner. The regular troops of the neighborhood of Moush were also attacked by these insurgents, who, however, did not dare to attack Moush itself, owing to the strong military forces of the town.

"The rebels, together with those assembled at Endouk-Dagh, organized then separate bands, which assisted ferociously the tribes close at hand, committing horrible crimes and depredations. They burned alive the nephew of Eumer Agha, and assaulted and murdered Mussulman women of three or four houses of the village of Gulli-Guzat. They also tortured many Muslims, forcing

71

them to kiss the cross, putting their eyes out, cutting their ears, and submitting them to the most horrible indignities.

"The same rebels, at the beginning of August last, attacked the tribes of Faninar of Bekiran, and of Badikan, committing crimes similar to the above. The insurgents of the villages of Ealighernuk, and of Yermouch, situated in the canton of Djinan (district of Calb), attacked in their turn the Kurds living there, as also the villages of Kaisser and of Tchatchat.

"Toward the end of August last, the Armenians were attacking the Kurds in the neighborhood of Moush, burning three or four villages, including Gulli-Guzat. In relation to the agitators of Talouri, numbering more than 3,000, after having brought consternation and death among Muslims and Christians alike, they refused to surrender, and continued their criminal proceedings. Regular troops were sent to that spot to put down their rebellion. The chief, Hampartzoum, fled to a high mountain with eleven of his associates in crime. He was captured alive, not, however, without his killing two soldiers and wounding six. By the end of August last all insurgent bands were dispersed.

"Women, children, and invalids were treated with due consideration, and according to the dictates of Islamism and humanity. The insurgents who fell were those who refused to surrender, and preferred to fight the lawful authorities of their country."

Those facts were subsequently corroborated by the testimony of an eye-witness, a Spanish traveler, and a Fellow of the Geographical Society of England, Mr. Ximenes, whose account of the Sassoun troubles was given in the following manner by the newspapers:

"Señor Ximenes, a well-known Spanish traveler, has just returned here after having completed a geographical mission for the Turkish government in Kurdistan and Mesopotamia, which lasted from March to November last. He happened to be in the Armenian province of Bitlis at the time of the alleged Sassoun disturbances, and he declares that he neither saw nor heard anything to warrant the sensational stories told of Armenian atrocities.

"Señor Ximenes remained a month at Constantinople, but while there he refused to discuss the matter in any form. He is now in London with Woods Pasha, and no longer has reason to remain silent. He is disposed to lay touch of the blame for the disturbed condition of Armenia on the American Methodist Missions in Asia Minor. He says that they give the Armenians a superficial education out of all proportion to the needs of the community. The pupils of these missions, he adds, are never satisfied to return to their homes and work their land. They continually speak of American liberty, and in nearly every case, says Señor Ximenes, the Armenian agitators are shown to have been pupils of the Methodist Missions.

"Señor Ximenes further declares that the statements that women and children were tortured and outraged by either the Turkish regulars or irregulars are untrue. The entire affair, the traveler insists, was limited to a local disturbance which was locally suppressed.

"After describing the troubles and fights between the Armenians and the Kurds early last summer, Señor Ximenes says that the Armenians gathered in large numbers in the Valley of Talari, near Sassoun. At the request of the Governor of Bitlis, orders were sent to Zekki Pasha to mobilize troops and restore order. Consequently, four battalions, about 1,200 men, were hastily collected and sent to disperse the Armenians. The troops overtook the latter on a plateau on August 28th, and demanded their surrender. The Armenians, who numbered about 3,000, commenced to jeer at the soldiers and pelt them with stones. The Armenians also fired several shots at the troops, and the latter replied with a volley. The Armenians then fled, and reassembled in a narrow valley, where the pursuing troops overtook them. The Turkish officer in command, in a conciliatory speech, advised them to disperse. Some obeyed, but many refused to do so, and the troops fired a second volley. In all, 300 Armenians were killed. This, according to Señor Ximenes, was the only serious affray of the whole affair. Many prisoners were taken, it is true, but they were afterwards released."

Now, as regards who were the true instigators, and who brought about such a state of things, nothing, we think, could be more acceptable to the English-speaking people than the statement of a man, who, like the Rev. Cyrus Hamlin, published, as far back as the 23rd of December, 1893, in *the Congregationalist*, the following remarkable letter:

"An Armenian 'revolutionary' party is causing great evil and suffering to the missionary work and to the whole Christian population of certain parts of the Turkish Empire. It is a secret organization, and is managed with a skill in deceit which is known only in the East.

"In a widely distributed pamphlet the following announcement is made at the close:

"'This is the only Armenian party which is leading on the revolutionary movement in Armenia. Its centre is Athens, and it has branches in every village and city in Armenia, also in the colonies. Nishan Garabedian, one of the founders of the party, is in America, and those desiring to get further information may communicate with him, addressing Nishan Garabedian, No. 15 Fountain Street, Worcester, Mass., or with the centre, M. Beniard, Poste Restante, Athens, Greece.'

"A very intelligent Armenian gentleman, who speaks fluently and correctly English, as well as Armenian, and is an eloquent defender of the revolution, assured me that they have the strongest hopes of preparing the way for Russia's entrance to Asia Minor to take possession. In answer to the question as to how, he replied: 'These Huntchaguist bands, organized all over the empire, will watch their opportunities to kill Turks and Kurds, set fire to their villages, and then make their escape into the mountains. The enraged Muslims will then rise and fall upon the defenseless Armenians, and slaughter them with such barbarities that Russia will enter, in the name of humanity and Christian civilization, and take possession.'

"When I denounced the scheme as atrocious and infernal beyond anything ever known, he calmly replied: 'It appears so to you, no doubt; but we Armenians are determined to be free. Europe listened to the Bulgarian horrors, and made Bulgaria free. She will listen to our cry when it goes up in the shrieks and blood of millions of women and children.' I urged in vain that this scheme will make the very name of Armenian hateful among all civilized people. He replied: 'We are desperate; we shall do it.'

"'But your people do not want Russian protection. They prefer Turkey, bad as she is. There are hundreds of miles of conterminous territory into which emigration is easy at all times. It has been so for all the centuries of Muslim rule. If your people preferred the Russian government, there would not be now an Armenian family in Turkey.'

"'Yes, 'he replied,' and for such stupidity they will have to suffer.'

"I have had conversations with others who avow the same things, but no one acknowledges that he is a member of the party. Falsehood is, of course, justifiable where murder and arson are.

"In Turkey the party aims to excite the Turks against Protestant missionaries and against Protestant Armenians. All the troubles at Marsovan originated in their movements. They are cunning, unprincipled, and cruel. They terrorize their own people by demanding contributions of money under threats of assassination — a threat which has often been put in execution.

"I have made the mildest possible disclosure of only a few of the abominations of this Huntchaguist revolutionary party. It is of Russian origin; Russian gold and craft govern it. Let all missionaries, home and foreign, denounce it. Let all Protestant Armenians everywhere boldly denounce it. It is trying to enter every Sunday school and deceive and pervert the innocent and ignorant into supporters of this craft. We must, therefore, be careful that in befriending Armenians we do nothing that can be construed into an approval of this movement, which all should abhor. While yet we recognize the probability that some Armenians in this country, ignorant of the real object and cruel designs of the Huntchaguists, are led by their patriotism to join with them, and while we sympathize with the sufferings of the Armenians at home, we must stand aloof from any such desperate attempts, which contemplate the destruction of Protestant missions, churches, schools, and Bible work, involving all in a common ruin that is diligently and craftily sought. Let ail home and foreign missionaries beware of any alliance with, or countenance of, the Huntchaguists.

"Cyrus Hamlin, Lexington, December 23."

To this prophetic letter may be added the following extracts taken from a letter of a special correspondent of the Associated Press. This correspondent is certainly not a friend of the Turks and of the Turkish Government, and yet he writes:

"It is a fact that certain of the Armenian conspirators arranged to murder the Rev. Edward Riggs and two other American missionaries at Marsovan and fasten the blame upon the Turks, in order that the United States might inflict summary punishment upon the Turkish Government, thereby making possible Armenian independence. One will search a long time in the pages of history for a more diabolical plot than that. Moreover, the missionaries would have been murdered had not an Armenian friend warned them. Dr. Riggs has unselfishly given his life to the education of Armenian youth in the missionary schools, and done more than any Armenian has ever tried to do towards making Armenians worthy of autonomous government. Yet the revolutionary conspirators apparently gave that fact little thought... It is, of course, impossible to say to what extent radical ideas prevail among the revolutionary propagandists, but the plans of some of the leaders are shocking in the extreme.

"In brief, their plans are to commit atrocities upon Turks in order that the infuriated Turks shall shock the Christian world by the fiendish outrages of their retaliation. When remonstrated with in regard to these un-Christian plans, the men who are responsible for them merely say: ' It may seem to you cruel and barbarous, but we know what we are doing and why we are doing it.'

"The financial methods of these men are almost as ingenious as their plans of political agitation. Certain Armenians of a lower grade of mental ability are required to furnish so many thousand piastres to the committee, and the means of obtaining the money are plainly mapped out. Here is a case in point:

"A wealthy Turk in the service of the Government in Constantinople received a letter one morning saying that unless he deposited 12,000 piastres in a certain place within twenty-four hours he would be killed. An investigation led to the discovery of the fact that the letter was written by an Armenian who had been in his employ as a trusted servant for several years. The servant confessed his guilt; but he asserted in self-defense that revolutionary agitators had compelled him to write the letter under penalty of death. It was a case of choice of wills, and the poor wretch saved his life at the expense of a long term of imprisonment. It is believed that a great deal of money is raised in this way, but whether or not this money gets beyond the pockets of the revolutionary agitators no man pretends to know. There is a theory that this money is used in the purchase of rifles and ammunition, but that is a matter known only to the agitators themselves."

Let any living being, after reading the above, maintain, with any semblance of truthfulness and common sense, that it is the Turkish government and the Turkish people who persecute the Armenians and endeavor to wipe out from the face of the earth their race and religion. It is, on the contrary, a fact that faithful and law-abiding Armenians are not only protected, but also employed in very high official positions, one of them even being, at the present moment, a Minister of the Imperial Crown. The fact is, also, that the Armenians in Turkey, numbering a little over 900,000 (for they are no more), have their own schools, that their language and literature are preserved, that their nationality is respected, that their leading men are promoted in the scale of high honors and positions, while Christian Europe and America have no care for the Jews, and while Catholic Spain has not allowed a single Muslim family to remain on its European territory, and has centuries ago expelled them all. The reason of this colossal difference lies in the fact that Islam is indeed a religion essentially and radically tolerant. If it were not, Turkey would not have had at the present moment a single Christian subject in any part of her vast dominions, and, for the benefit of the Turks, there would not exist now what is called the Eastern question. Turks suffer in our days from the tolerance that forms an intrinsic and essential part of their religion. Europe and America ought to be thankful to them. Instead of that, we see not a few eloquent Christian fanatics who countenance in Turkey what certainly they would not encourage in their own countries, namely, insubordination and revolt. Is this justice?

The same spirit of injustice to Turkey is shown in regard to the policy of Turkey toward the Armenians naturalized in the United States on their return to the country of their birth, and many unfair accusations arc made against the Sublime Porte for its insisting, in the absence of any naturalization treaty between Turkey and America, upon applying a law which is both wise and necessary, and which had been promulgated long before these Armenian troubles had begun. A short statement of facts as they really are, and not as disguised by Turkey's detractors, will, it is trusted, be deemed useful for the understanding of the case.

The law concerning Ottoman naturalization is dated 19th of January, 1869, and is as follows:

Article 1 — "Every person born of Ottoman father and mother, or only of an Ottoman father, is an Ottoman subject.

Article 2 — "Every person born on Ottoman territory, of foreign parents, may, within three years after attaining majority, claim as of right the character of an Ottoman subject.

Article 3 — "Every major foreigner who has resided during five consecutive years in the Ottoman empire, may obtain Ottoman nationality by applying, directly or through an intermediary, to the minister of foreign affairs.

Article 4 — "The Imperial Government may, by extraordinary act, confer Ottoman nationality on the foreigner who, without having fulfilled the conditions of the preceding article, should be deemed worthy of this exceptional favor.

Article 5 — "The Ottoman subject who has acquired a foreign nationality with the authorization of the Imperial Government, is considered and treated as a foreign subject; if, on the contrary, he is naturalized as a foreigner, without the previous authorization of the Imperial Government, his naturalization shall be considered as null and of no effect, and he will continue to be considered and treated in all respects as an Ottoman subject.

"No Ottoman subject can, in any case, naturalize himself as a foreigner, except after having obtained a certificate of authorization issued in virtue of an Imperial irade.

Article 6 — "Nevertheless, the Imperial Government may declare loss of the character of an Ottoman subject, against any Ottoman subject who shall have naturalized himself in a foreign country, or who shall have accepted military functions under a foreign government, without the authorization of his sovereign.

"In this case the loss of the character of an Ottoman subject shall entail, ipso facto, the interdiction of the return to the Ottoman Empire of the person who shall have incurred it.

Article 7 — "The Ottoman woman who has married a foreigner, may, if she become a widow, recover her character of an Ottoman subject by making declaration to that end within three years following the decease of her husband. This provision is, however, only applicable to her person. Her property shall be subject to the laws and general regulations controlling the same.

Article 8 — "The child, even when a minor, of an Ottoman subject who has naturalized himself as a foreigner, who has lost his nationality, does not follow the status of his father, and remains an Ottoman subject. The child, even when a minor, of a foreigner who has naturalized himself an Ottoman, does not follow the status of his father, and remains a foreigner.

Article 9 — "Every person inhabiting the Ottoman territory is reputed an Ottoman subject, and treated as such, until his character as a foreigner shall have been regularly proved."

The contents of this law were interpreted, and its real meaning clearly defined to the governors-general of all the provinces of the empire by the following Vizirial circular, dated 26th of March, 1869:

"I have personally transmitted to you the law of Ottoman nationality, promulgated on the 6th *Cheval*, 1285 (January 19, 1869). While this law in its context cannot give rise to divergent interpretations, I deem it important to define to you the spirit which inspired its most important provisions.

"I need not, in the first place, say to you that this law, like any other law, has no retroactive effect; all who have already been admitted to Ottoman nationality, and all native Ottoman subjects who have, either by virtue of treaties, or by virtue of special arrangements concluded between the Sublime Porte and the foreign missions accredited to it, been recognized by the Imperial Government as having acquired a foreign nationality, remain, as heretofore, either Ottoman or foreign subjects.

"The provisions set forth in Articles 1, 2, 3, and 4 are plain enough to make any comment unnecessary. I shall merely remind you that since the 'personal' law of each individual, that is, the law of the country of his origin, is that which determines the time of his majority, and since that law varies according to countries, the majority being reached in some countries at twenty-five years and above, and below that age in others; it will be incumbent on all foreign subjects who may apply for Ottoman naturalization to prove that they are of age according to the law of the country of their origin.

"Article 5 imposes on all Ottoman subjects who wish to acquire a foreign nationality, the obligation of previously providing themselves with a written authorization, which will be delivered to them by virtue of an imperial irade, without which their naturalization shall always be considered as void and of no effect, and the Imperial Government will even have it in its power (Art. 6) to declare them divested of the character of Ottoman subjects, which will, *ipso facto*, entail the interdiction of returning to the Ottoman empire. The application of the penalty provided for in Article 6, exclusively appertains to the Imperial Government. Imperial authorities will confine themselves to considering as void and of no effect foreign naturalization when acquired without previous authorization by a native Ottoman subject, and will take no steps looking to expulsion, without having first received direct instructions from the Sublime Porte.

"'Inasmuch as the Ottoman woman who marries an alien ceases to be an Ottoman subject, she is granted, under Article 7, the faculty of recovering her original nationality, in the event of her becoming a widow, by so declaring to the Ottoman authority within three years after her husband's decease.

"Article 8 establishes that the father's naturalization does not carry that of his children, even though these be minors. The benefit of naturalization, when granted to the father, is not extended to his children, except so far as they wish it. If they are of age, they are at liberty to follow the father's status by making application therefore; if not, they may do so as soon as they reach their majority. It is easy to understand that this provision, which is, besides, in conformity with that of the greater part of European legislation, is enacted for the very advantage of the children, who may occasionally find inconvenience or even detriment to themselves in their father's naturalization.

"However, this provision does not apply to children born subsequently to the father's naturalization. These follow their father's status, and form part of the nation to which they belong, in consequence of his naturalization.

"The last clause of the law exclusively bears on the case of individuals who may, for good reasons, be thought to be Ottoman subjects, and would claim a foreign nationality without being in a position to support their claim. It is obvious that, in the event of dispute, it is incumbent on him who claims foreign nationality to adduce evidence thereof; and until such evidence is produced, the Imperial authorities must, inasmuch as he is found on Ottoman territory, consider him and treat him as an Ottoman subject.

"It is needless to add that Article 8 affects in no way the rights secured by treaties to foreigners, and docs not justify the Imperial authorities in departing from the regulations resulting from such treaties regarding their relations with foreigners.

"I shall close, Mr. Governor-General, in bringing to your notice the fact that naturalization cannot, under any circumstances, have for effect to free the naturalized person from civil or criminal proceedings that may have been instituted against him prior to the time when he was naturalized, before the authority of which he was a dependent theretofore.

"You will please, Mr. Governor-General, to strictly conform to these instructions in enforcing the provisions of the new law. With a view to facilitating your duties, this communication will also be sent to the foreign nations accredited to the Sublime Porte, in order that it may be brought to the notice of their agents in the provinces."

Armenians and their friends in America have witnessed publicly that the law, a copy of which has just been given, is applicable solely to Armenians, and to Armenians naturalized in no other country but in the United States. The very perusal of the law shows these accusations to be meant to misguide public opinion. The law is for all former Turkish subjects, with no reference to their nationality and creed, who might have been naturalized either in the United States or in any country in Europe. Armenians, however, have no wish to seek for a European naturalization. The reason is threefold: First, Europe knows well the Armenians, while America does not. Second, the endeavors made by American missionaries to convert the Armenians, and to give them a certain education, considered by Mr. Ximenes as inimical to the Turkish government, prompt the latter to give their preference to the United States. Third, Armenians consider the American law on naturalization more advantageous to their secret plans and intentions, for American passports do not, for instance, contain the following clause, that is always to be found on English passports:

> "This passport is granted with the qualification that the bearer shall not, when within the limits of the foreign state of which he was a subject previously to obtaining his certificate of naturalization, be deemed to be a British subject, unless he has ceased to be a subject of that state, in pursuance of the laws thereof, or in pursuance of a treaty to that effect."

If such a wise clause were put on all American passports, Armenians who wish now to become American citizens, in order to hide themselves behind the protection of the United States government, would very promptly abandon American citizenship altogether, to the great relief of the State Department of Washington. The proof that Armenians almost never get naturalized in good faith, but, with perhaps no exception, in order to make use, if possible, of the United States government against Turkey, is shown by the following extract of an official report of the present able United States Minister at Constantinople, Mr. Alexander Terrell, who, under date of 29th of September, 1893, writes:

> "The European emigrant in the United States generally naturalizes in good faith: the Asiatic very rarely does. I am in a position to know that it is the rule, rather than the exception, that the Armenian returns soon after he is naturalized, and goes back with the intention of remaining."

The statement was made above that American missionaries' side, on the whole, with Armenian revolutionists against Turkey. This statement is based on the written declarations made lately by the American Board of Commissioners for Foreign Missions, who, instead of advising the Armenians to be law-abiding subjects of the Sultan, and to preserve a dignified silence until the result of the investigation about the Sassoun troubles is made known, considered more to the point to affirm the existence of cold-blooded massacres, when that Board ought to have known that no cold-blooded massacres of any kind are countenanced by the Turkish government, and that the very presence in Turkey of American missionaries and American schools, missionaries and schools existing principally for the conversion of Armenians to Protestantism, proved beyond doubt the tolerant spirit of the Turkish institutions. If American missionaries continue to side with discontented Armenians in Turkey, they will follow a policy contrary to the wish of the American government and people. Turkey, at all events, must have peace at all cost in her own possessions. She cannot allow foreign intrigues on her territory, and she is justified in resenting the following admission made by an Armenian about the participation of Americans in the Bulgarian affairs of 1875:

> "I see of late [writes that Armenian to the 'Boston Herald'], Rev. Cyrus Hamlin has been writing letters of sympathy and support to the various meetings held in this country in behalf of the Armenians, in unmistakable terms as to his present attitude toward their cause. Several years ago I heard him lecture at Amherst, Mass. How proud he was to tell his audience the important part taken by the Bulgarian graduates of Robert College in securing the freedom and independence of their country! I ask Rev Cyrus Hamlin if he was not aware of the existence of patriotic societies among his Bulgarian students, etc."

According to a French saying, we are only betrayed by our friends. Let American missionaries and their Board realize that it is not their duty and mission to help in "securing the freedom and independence" of any nationality in Turkey, or to countenance secret societies, or to accuse before the world the Turkish government of massacres that have not and cannot have any existence in reality. Their duty is simple enough. It consists in confining their policy and utterances to the strict observance of the laws of the country that gives them hospitality. While, therefore, it is to be wondered why American Missionaries, instead of devoting all their energies and good intentions on American Indians or on American negroes, choose to go to Turkey to educate in a certain fashion, and to convert, if possible, Christian Armenians to Protestantism; and while it is a fact that the Sublime Porte, thanks to the teachings of tolerance of its predominant religion, is willing to allow them, under its laws, to pursue their work ; no one in all fairness could blame Turkey for manifesting uneasiness for the public utterances and written statements inimical to her government, made lately by the Board of said missionaries, and tending fatally to encourage farther revolt and further disturbances on her territory. The United States would certainly not allow such a guilty manifestation on the part of any foreign missionaries that might come here to educate and convert our Indians, for example, especially if the latter were implicated, as Armenians acknowledge themselves to be, in revolutionary schemes. What is right for the United States, why should it not be right for Turkey? The Armenian agitation, based on falsehoods and exaggerations, and also on a pre arranged plan, as described by Rev. Cyrus Hamlin himself, has been supported and intensified by many people for the only reason that the Armenians are Christians, which fact tends to prove that mere fanaticism animates Turkey's detractors. If this were not the case, the irresponsible and wild allegations of revolutionary Armenians would never have been believed and commented upon by people who call themselves impartial, without corresponding and convincing proofs. Turkey, therefore, sees now that she cannot implicitly rely on impartiality and on justice. But she knows that she can rely on her sovereign. She is proud of him for having reorganized her finances, put her army on a very high level, and introduced wise reforms in every branch of her administration. She admires his wonderful energy, superior intelligence, and generous heart. She is well aware that under him she has nothing to fear either from foreign or from internal foes, and it is because Turkey's belief is based upon facts that Sultan Abdul Hamid II is truly a great monarch.

# The Armenian Troubles
## and
## Where the Responsibilities Lie

The five letters now published in this pamphlet were originally reproduced by an influential newspaper of New York. They were written at and sent from Constantinople, where impartial and correct information was accessible. The author, in republishing these letters, together with further evidence, has only one wish in view, and that is to impart to his readers a true and thorough knowledge of the present Armenian troubles. He believes that the whole atmosphere on this subject has been polluted with falsehoods and exaggerations, and trusts that the present short and condensed pamphlet will help in bringing some light on a question so often misrepresented.

# Letter One

The Turkish Government has never denied that serious disturbances have taken place at the district of Sassoun. What it has denied is the accusation that there was a premeditated massacre; and yet this is the absurd basis upon which is built the whole Armenian agitation, both in America and Europe. The mere idea that the Sultan would order a massacre of his Christian subjects, Armenians or no Armenians, is ridiculous in itself, and denotes a credulous belief in the falsehoods and calumnies propagated by the Armenian revolutionary committees.

People cannot understand here in Turkey how serious American newspapers could accept and print in their columns assertions made with the object of throwing odium on the legitimate authority of a friendly power. Mere affirmations ought not to be considered as sufficient. Proof ought to be asked above everything else. If such were the case, the most wild absurdities about Turkey would never appear in the daily press. What, however has surprised some people most is to see the boldness and fanaticism of not a few American clergymen, who try to impart a religious and fanatical tendency to a question that is, and ought to remain, a political one.

That Turkey does not make any religious distinctions between her subjects is shown by the fact that Armenians, who, as a race, are certainly much inferior to the Turks, occupy very high positions in Turkey. While this is the case with Islamic Turkey, may we ask who are the Christian governments that reward their Jewish subjects, for example, with corresponding honors and influence? And yet the Jewish race is indeed a great one, for it has left a mark in the history of mankind.

What Turkey wants is peace, and she is determined to have it. The Sassoun disturbances were brought about by Armenian revolutionary committees. Turkey as an independent State had to put down these disturbances. She did it with a severity less great than the one displayed by England under similar circumstances. As regards now the demand for reforms, let it be remembered that reforms are needed in every country, and not in Turkey alone. We have not heard that the Irish question has been solved, and yet nobody recommends to England to abandon her sovereign rights and independence. Turkey will stick to the same rule, for she has the same rights and the same independence.   In the meanwhile, it would be well for American public opinion, instead of showing an implicit faith in Armenian falsehoods, to let these Armenian Christians know that they ought, for their own sake, to abandon their seditious agitation.   The rest will necessarily follow.

# Letter Two

In our previous letter we affirmed that the Sassoun troubles were brought about by the criminal efforts of Armenian revolutionary committees, and that no reliance whatever ought to be placed on Armenian testimony and assertions. We now propose to prove these two affirmations, not by Turkish- that is to say, Muslim - testimony, but by American and European: namely, Christian testimony.

The man who, above all, gave the most explicit and true account of the Armenian revolutionary movement is Rev. Cyrus Hamlin himself. On the 23rd of December, 1893, or, in other words, only a few months before the revolt of Sassoun, he published in the Congregationalist a truly prophetic statement, the perusal of which is absolutely necessary for an impartial understanding of the case. Here is this statement:

> "An Armenian 'revolutionary' party is causing great evil and suffering to the missionary work and to the whole Christian population of certain parts of the Turkish Empire. It is a secret organization, and is managed with a skill which is known only in the East. In a widely distributed pamphlet the following announcement is made at the close:
>
> "'This is the only Armenian party which is leading on the revolutionary movement in Armenia. Its centre in Athens, and it has branches in every village and city in Armenia, also in the colonies. Nishan Garabedian, 15 Fountain Street, Worcester, Mass., or with the centre, M. Beniard, Poste Restante, Athens, Greece.'
>
> "When I denounced the scheme as atrocious and infernal beyond anything ever known, he calmly replied: 'It appears so to you, no doubt, but we Armenians are determined to be free. Europe listened to the Bulgarian horrors, and made Bulgaria free. She will listen to our cry when it goes up in the shrieks and blood of millions of women and children.' I urged in vain that this scheme would make the very name of Armenian hateful among all civilized people. He relied: 'We are desperate; we shall do it.' 'But your people do not want Russian protection. They prefer Turkey, bad as she is. There are hundreds of miles of conterminous territory into which emigration is easy at

all times. It has been so for all centuries of Muslim rule. If your people preferred the Russian Government, there would not now be an Armenian family in Turkey.' 'Yes,' he replied, 'and for such stupidity they will have to suffer.'

"I have had conversations with others who avow the same things, but no one acknowledged that he is a member of the party. Falsehood is, of course, justifiable where murder and arson are. In Turkey the party aims to excite the Turks against Protestant missionaries and against Protestant Armenians. All the trouble at Marsovan originated in their movements. They are cunning, unprincipled, and cruel. They terrorize their own people by demanding contributions of money under threats of assassination - a threat which has often been put into execution.

"I have made the mildest possible disclosure of only a few of the abominations of this Huntchaguist revolutionary party. It is of Russian origin; Russian gold and craft govern it. Let all missionaries, home and foreign, denounce it. Let all Protestant Armenians everywhere boldly denounce it. It is trying to enter every Sunday-school and deceive and pervert the innocent and ignorant into supporters of this craft. We must, therefore, be careful that in befriending Armenians we do nothing that can be construed into an approval of this movement, which all should abhor. While yet we recognize the probability that some Armenians in this country, ignorant of the real object and cruel designs of the Huntchaguists, are led by their patriotism to join with them, and while we sympathize with the sufferings of the Armenians at home, we must stand aloof from any such desperate attempts, which contemplate the destruction of Protestant missions, churches, schools, and Bible work, involving all in a common ruin that is diligently and craftily sought. Let all home and foreign missionaries beware of any alliance with, or countenance of, the Huntchaguists."

No one really knows whether the Rev. Cyrus Hamlin is considered to be a prophet in his own country, but his prophetic faculties as far as the last Armenian revolt is concerned are not denied in Turkey. They are simply marvelous; for, months before the occurrence of the Sassoun troubles, the rev. Cyrus Hamlin was bold enough to say that the above statement was written by him only "to show the absurdity of the revolutionary plotters." The reverend gentleman must have a candid and innocent soul. Otherwise he would not have attempted to prove to fair-minded Americans that the "bloodthirstiness" of the Armenian revolutionary plotters is synonymous with their "absurdity." We suppose that the "absurdity of revolutionary plotters" the following statement, showing his past guilty interference in Turkish affairs. One of these Armenian "plotters" made some time ago in the Boston Herald this extraordinary admission, which, for the honor of Robert College, if not for his own, the Rev. Cyrus Hamlin ought, if he can, to contradict:

> "Several years ago," writes the Armenian, "I heard him lecture at Amherst, Massachusetts. How proud he was to tell the audience the important part taken by the Bulgarian graduates of Robert College in securing the freedom and independence of their country! I ask the Rev. Cyrus Hamlin if he was not aware of the existence of patriotic societies among his Bulgarian students," etc.

But in order to show that the Rev. Cyrus Hamlin's prophecy holds good, let American readers reflect on the following passage of a letter written by the special correspondent of the Associated Press, who visited Turkey after the Sassoun revolt, and who, although bitterly opposed to the Turkish Government, wrote as follows:

> "It is a fact that certain of the Armenian conspirators arranged to murder the Rev. Edward Riggs and two other American missionaries at Marsovan and fasten the blame upon the Turkish Government, thereby making possible Armenian independence. One will search a long time in the pages of history for a more diabolical plot than that. Moreover, the missionaries would have been murdered had not an Armenian friend warned them. Dr. Riggs has unselfishly given his life to the education of Armenian youth in the missionary schools, and done more

than any Armenian has ever tried to do toward making Armenians worthy of autonomous government. Yet the revolutionary conspirators apparently gave that little thought.... It is, of course, impossible to say to what extent radical ideas prevail among the revolutionary propagandists, but the plans of some of the leaders are shocking to the extreme.

"In brief, their plans are to commit atrocities upon Turks, in order that the infuriated Turks shall shock the Christian world by the fiendish outrages of their retaliations. When remonstrated with in regard to these un-Christian plans, the men who are responsible for them merely say: 'It may seem to you cruel and barbarous, but we know what we are doing, and why we are doing it.'

"The financial methods of these men are almost as ingenious as their plans of political agitation. Certain Armenians of a lower grade of mental ability are required to furnish so many thousands of piastres to the committee, and the means of obtaining the money are plainly mapped out. Here is a case in point.

"A wealthy Turk in the service of the Government in Constantinople received a letter one morning, saying that unless he deposited 12,000 piastres in a certain place within twenty-four hours he would be killed. An investigation led to the discovery of the fact that the letter was written by an Armenian who had been in his employ as a trusted servant for several years. The servant confessed his guilt, but he asserted in self-defense that revolutionary agitators had compelled him to write the letter under penalty of death. It was a case of choice of wills, and the poor wretch saved his life at the expense of a long term of imprisonment. It is believed that a great deal of money is raised in that way, but whether or not this money gets beyond the pockets of the revolutionary agitators, no man pretends to know. There is a theory that this money is used in the purchase of rifles and ammunition, but that is a matter known only to the agitators themselves."

The reason why English public opinion is generally in favor of the Armenians is both political and religious. No real esteem for the Armenians themselves exists in England. Besides, everybody admits in Europe that Armenians are, as a race, much inferior to the Turks. Armenians, even in olden times, showed no greatness. Their influence in the world has been absolutely nil. In science, in art, in literature, in war-like achievements, they have left no trace. But they are Christians; and this is one reason why English popular opinion is in their favor. The political reason lies in the fact that England wishes to harass Turkey for the just opposition of the latter to English scandalous encroachments on Egyptian territory, which, after all, belongs legitimately to the Sultan. It is just as if England had taken possession of one of the American States, and at the same time were fomenting discontent for, and disapprobation of, the treatment of the Indian race which Columbus found supreme on this continent.

Such being the real state of things, we consider that it is quite time for public opinion in the United States to see how erroneous and even anti American is the policy which consists in helping England in her political aspirations in the East. American public opinion ought to remain aloof from European intrigues. It ought especially to learn to estimate correctly the value of Armenian assertions and of the Armenian moral standard.

"If," writes the Associated Press correspondent above quoted, "the detailed facts of the Sassoun massacre are ever established, it must be independently of Armenian testimony, or their value may be seriously questioned. In the first place, every Armenian with whom it has been my lot to come in contact seems to have a very vague idea as to the value of truth. In the second place, in his anxiety to make out a case against the Turk, he is willing to publish as fact any grotesque rumor that he may chance to fall over in the street. In the third place, he does not really know what actually took place in the Sassoun mountains, but his vanity will not permit him to acknowledge it, and so, to be up with the times and to help along the cause of his people, he embellishes the rumor that he hears, and frequently says that he is in secret communications with friends in Moosh and Bitlis, who are harboring Sassoun refugees. The average Armenian cannot be believed on oath."

In this deplorable condition of Armenian honesty, we find a true explanation of the following remarkable incident, an account of which was given at the time, as follows, by all the newspapers:

> "The story which has been thrilling the world for some time past, of the wife of the Armenian leader Grego, who, rather than suffer dishonor at the hands of her Turkish persecutors, threw herself, with her child in her arms, into an abyss, and was followed by other women until the ravine was filled with corpses, has been exploded, as many persons predicted it would be, at the time it was sprung upon the public. It has been discovered that the horrible narrative is a reproduction, with additions and embellishments to suit the occasion, of an old tale told in poetry by Mrs. Hemans years ago, under the title of 'The Suliote Mother.'"

In the face of all the innumerable Armenian falsehoods of this kind, word has just reached us that Mr. Gladstone, in his Chester speech, asserted that the world is in possession of independent American testimony favorable to the Armenians. No greater error has ever been made. Mr. Gladstone ought to have known better. There is absolutely no American testimony regarding the Sassoun troubles. And the reason is very simple. No American was at the Sassoun district at the time of the revolt. The Rev. F.D. Greene, it is true, published a slanderous pamphlet on the "Armenian Crisis in Turkey," in which he printed a few documents supposed to he well authenticated. But as no American born citizen saw anything of the Sassoun disturbances, it follows necessarily that said documents were written either by Armenians or by American missionaries, under the inspiration of Armenians. Therefore the Rev. F.D. Greene's pamphlet is based upon Armenian falsehoods. This makes it utterly and completely valueless. Mr. Gladstone owes to us to show where and how he was able to find a single genuine American document favoring the Armenian allegations; that is to say, the allegations of a people who "cannot be believed on oath." Facts, however, have very seldom disturbed Mr. Gladstone's fanaticism. We trust that Americans, having no political views on Turkey, will see how dangerous it is to encourage either by word or by moral help, Armenian revolutionaries the simple reason that they are Christians.

"Armenia," wrote some time ago the correspondent mentioned above, "is preparing for war. The revolutionary party, as now both money and guns. During the past eight weeks money has poured into the revolutionary treasury in a steady stream from the Armenian colonies in Batoum, Tiflis, Baku, Erivan, Etchmiadzin, and other places in Russia, and from Rescht, Kazvin, Teheran, Tebriz, Khoi, and other cities in Persia. I have not visited the Armenian colonies on the north coast of the Black Sea, nor the large colony at Isfahan in Southern Persia, but I am reliably informed that revolutionary agents have been as busy there as elsewhere. I have myself seen a considerable sum of this money raised publicly, and I am told that the wealthy Armenian merchants in the cities I have named have made large private contributions, with promises of more for future use if needed.

> "The money raised publicly has been obtained by means of balls, social entertainments, theatrical performances and lotteries. These functions were ostensibly for the 'benefit of the Sassoun refugees.' But it was a very thin disguise. It was thoroughly understood what the money was wanted for, and that the Sassoun refugees would not see a penny of it except in the shape of rifles and ammunition."

The cries, therefore in favor of the Sassoun refugees and the famished are either based on Armenian falsehoods or uttered by those who have political aims to further and attain. Could Americans be deceived by such a very "thin disguise"? We doubt it.

# Letter Three

LORD SALISBURY'S assertion in his speech on the address namely, that Turkey's independence "exists by reason of the agreement of other powers that they will not interfere with it, and that they will maintain it" may sound well to the ears of Turkey's detractors, but, if true, the same assertion may also be considered as applying with equal force to every power on earth. And the reason is simple enough. Suppose, for argument's sake, that the European powers, one and all, were to combine their forces, by land as well as by sea, and, with a unity that necessarily would become overwhelming, were to fall upon all British possessions: where would the "independence" of the British Empire be? No doubt it would speedily vanish.

An "agreement," therefore, tacit or not tacit, always exists between civilized nations, an agreement the purport of which is that they will not "interfere" with each others "independence," and that they will "maintain" it. Otherwise there would be no stability in human affairs no political life among nations, no progress. Now, Lord Salisbury may think, if he chooses, that England is an unassailable power, whose first serious defeat from a coming foe would not be the certain signal of her collapse and dismemberment. He may assert that Turkey is, on the contrary, a vulnerable power. But let him ask the Russians what they think of the Turkish soldiers. Let the whole world answer to this. Turkey's "independence" is as certain as England's. To break down her "independence" Turkey's enemies must fight first. Words are misleading when they do not correspond to facts.

It seems, however as if Lord Salisbury had lost the memory of some facts especially concerning English cruelty. His non reference to the Indian mutiny of 1857, and his abstaining to compare it with the Sassoun revolt were most characteristic. Anybody who knows anything about English history and English tenderness of heart remembers with what savage cruelty, with what streams of blood, the English soldiery put down the rebellion of that year. Even Armenian falsehoods as applied to Sassoun were below the truth in comparison with the English application in India of an imperial policy of extermination and death. Such words as "butchery," "hellish deeds," "piteous moans," "piercing cries," "shrieks," "screams," "vain voices of blood and agony," and the like, that fill Dr. Dillon's article on Turkey which has just appeared in an English magazine, apply a thousand times more to the British repression or the Indian mutiny of 1857 than to the Turkish repression of the Armenian revolt of Sassoun of 1894.

Even to day, if there were to manifest itself in India an agitation equal to the one described by the Rev. Cyrus Hamlin himself as having existed eighteen months ago in Asiatic Turkey among Armenians, the same English soldiery would use absolutely the same cruel means for preserving the "integrity" of the British Empire. And yet no Christian power would think of raising its voice against such a policy. No public meetings would take place in America to condemn a Protestant country. The past has shown us that such would be the case. And even in the present time, who in Europe or in the United States sends a word of sympathy to those Muslims, to those Muslim women and children, to those Muslim villages that are being plundered and outraged by savage Bulgarians?

Whatever the cause of this conduct may be, nothing, we consider, will be found more instructing and more edifying than the perusal of a remarkable letter published by Mrs. S. L. Baldwin, in the New York Tribune. Every impartial American will surely judge Turkey with more charity after reading the following passages of said letter:

> "Let us be correct and fair in our records. There is cause for us Americans not to be too free with our exhortations, epithets, and threats. The Chinese are not sinners above all others. If you will grant me space in your paper, I will give you reliable details of such outrages against the Chinese in the United States- not in the interior cities, but that have taken place in Boston, New York, and Brooklyn, as well as in San Francisco, San Jose, Sacramento, Tacoma, Denver, Seattle, and other places - that at least ought to make us silent as well as sad in our present grief over the Ku-Cheng cablegram. I know of no terrible massacre in China in 1885; but I can give the most horrible details of one that occurred right here in our honorable (?) country. I had the painful duty of writing the only detailed account of it published in the East, and had to lay down my pen and leave my desk three times before I

could go through with it. I had the triple official documents - Chinese, United States, and Union Pacific Railroad - from which to make my painful, reliable record.

"In that massacre, which does distinguish 1885 in our history, more Chinese were killed, shot down, burned alive, in one awful hour, that day in September at Rock Spring, Wyoming, than were English and Americans killed in China in twenty-five years. For the Ku-Cheng outrage men will be arrested and executed, officers will be removed and degraded, and all property will be made good. For the Rock Springs massacre of fifty perfectly innocent people - so all authorities, our own Messrs. Cleveland and Bayard among them, declared- up to this date of August 6, 1895, no human being has been arrested, much less punished. All the hard-earned gains of these fifty people were stolen or destroyed, for which our highest authorities declared that 'in justice' there was no claim for indemnity, but 'ex-gratia' it might be given; but even 'ex-gratia' it was not granted until, a few years later, our own West China Mission was raided - no one hurt - and we wanted $25,000 for our destroyed property, and our Government had enough shame left to hurry up and pay the 'ex-gratia' sum before it shook the American flag before the Chinese Government - so infamous- did not right our fearful wrongs, and ' in justice,' not 'ex-gratia,' pay up quickly! Again I say, let us be fair!

"I conclude with a question: Is it a greater offence to 'Our Father' for His American, English, and French children to be killed in China than His Chinese children to come to a like tragic end in the United States? If an offender's sin is to be judged by the fight he has, what must the answer be? I am in deep grief for the beloved friends thrust out of life in Ku-Cheng, and I am and have been these many years in as great sorrow for my Chinese friends so brutally robbed and killed in this land filled with gospel light."

# Letter Four

Word has just reached here from Kara-Hissari-Charki that a band of Armenians attacked Nedjib Effendi, substitute to the Attorney-General, when on his way to Sivas, accompanied by gendarmes and by Rami Effendi, chief of the correspondence at Tchoroun. Rami Effendi, as well as the gendarmes, were dangerously wounded, while Nedjib Effendi was carried to the woods and murdered.

It is by deeds similar to the above that Armenian revolutionists, according to their own admission, expect again to bring about very serious troubles in Asiatic Turkey. In addition to the above, it may, perhaps, be of interest to give also the following facts, taken out of many, and showing the criminal work of the Armenian revolutionary committees:

1. An Armenian priest, suspected of spying, was quite recently murdered at Scutari, just opposite Constantinople, by Armenian agents of the revolutionary party.

2. Thirteen pupils of the American College at Marsovan, having been expelled last year because their fathers were suspected of being mixed up in the Armenian movement, suspicion has fallen on the college, and among the list of persons condemned by the Armenian committee are five professors of the college, two being Americans.

3. An Armenian named Garabed Agha was assassinated at Marsovan, close to the church door, as he was going to attend early service. He was the chief man of the Protestant community, and Chairman of the Council of Thirty, which is responsible for the peace of the city. It was alleged that he had given the Government information in regard to the revolutionists.

Commenting on the murder of Garabed Agha, the Rev. George E. White, an American missionary at the Congregational School at Marsovan, wrote as follows:

> "There are two parties of Armenians. Same say: 'We must be loyal to the Turkish Government. We cannot effect a revolution. We are to few.' Others say: ' We will assassinate and stir up until we overturn this Turkish Government.' And these revolutionists are ready to kill any of their brother Armenians or missionaries who do not help

on the rebellion. They killed Garabed Agha because he would not help the rebellion."

4. The Rev. Dr. Dwight, a leading American missionary, made recently the following statement, which shows not only what Armenian agitation means, but also the praiseworthy efforts of some Turkish Governors tending to prevent the outbreak of a fresh Armenian revolt:

"More than a year ago," said the Rev. Dr. Dwight, "sixteen persons at Marsovan received written notice that they would be killed unless they would cooperate with the Armenian revolutionists. President Tracey and Professor Riggs, of Marsovan College, were two of these. They had incurred the ill-will of the revolutionists by refusing to receive in the college the sons of certain men suspected of being revolutionists. Garabed Agha and another man were two of the sixteen who received notice, and both were assassinated. A Turkish guard was furnished, at the request of Mr. Terrell, to protect the American families from the assassins. The local governor informed the Armenians, after the killing, that he intended to arrest all suspected persons: that their object was to provoke Turkish vengeance in order to secure the sympathy and intervention of Christian Europe, but that they would not succeed, as he had caused to be preached in the mosques for months that such was their object, and that any Turk who killed a Christian would be the worst enemy of Islam."

5. The Rev. James I. Barton, one of the Secretaries of the American Board of Commissioners for Foreign Missions, reported the following incident:

"At the graduation exercises at the American College at Karpoot, after the distribution of diplomas, it was intended by the Faculty to have an address read thanking the Sultan, in the name of the people of Karpoot. The address was to have been read by an Armenian graduate. When the Armenians heard that the address was in their name, they protested, and warned the student who was to read it that if he did so he would lose his life. This made him afraid, and he refused to deliver the address. At last the American missionaries prevailed upon an Armenian teacher, Nigoghoss Tenekejian, to read it. When the day selected arrived, and as the teacher rose to speak, the populace began to sing the most radical of all Armenian revolutionary songs. The uproar was so great that the missionaries could not get the address read. The day following the incident, ten shots were fired into the house of the Armenian member of the college, and a placard placed on his door which read: 'If you continue your present course, be sure your life will be taken away.'"

Facts like the above have opened the eyes and aroused the indignation of unprejudiced men of all countries. But no more able description of that feeling of indignation can be found than in the following passage of a fearless American newspaper the perusal of which will surely give satisfaction to the sense of justice of many impartial readers:

"It appears that the Armenian conspirators are ready to threaten, or, if need be, to assassinate, all who refuse to join in their conspiracy, and that from this scheme of violence they exclude neither their own people nor the American missionaries who have gone to Asia Minor to labor for their advancement. They have already murdered a number of Armenians, many of them priests, and it is no longer a secret that they have threatened the lives of American missionaries whom they suspect of a lack of sympathy with their plans of bloodshed and disorder. The truth appears to be, as The Post has insisted all along, that the whole trouble is due to the Armenian incendiaries and to their programme of organized agitation. Thousands of intelligent and law abiding Armenians dwell peacefully in Turkey, receiving the impartial protection of the law. They practically control the commerce of the country; they are bankers, merchants, professional men; they hold office under the government, and are esteemed and respected accordingly. But these pestiferous firebrands- meaning the desperate criminals who make the trouble at home, and their accomplices in England and America who distort and misrepresent the facts to prejudice the outside world against Turkey- these indefatigable criminals whom we are now beginning to see in their true colors, deserve no sympathy from civilized people anywhere, and should not be permitted to mislead honest men with their falsehoods and their impudent pretensions."

But Turkey's detractors insist that there was a premeditated massacre ac Sassoun. They willingly and intentionally leave aside the fact that the Armenian committees were the real instigators of a serious revolt there, which had to be put down by the Turkish Government. All Christian governments, like Russia, England, and even the United States, surely had at times to employ brutal force in order to suppress disturbances and rebellion.

When the great "de Maistre" was asked why he showed such an earnest opposition to the abolition of capital punishment, he answered by these words:

"Que Messieurs les assassins commencent!" In the same way, let Armenian committees cease their criminal intrigues and assassinations; let them abandon revolt, and, soon enough, repression on the part of the Turkish Government will stop. What Armenians need most at the present moment is, we think, good advice. What they get is, unfortunately, bad advice. We consider, for instance, as constituting very bad advice, all the hatred, all the exaggerations, all the slanders that abound in the Rev. Frederick Davis Greene's pamphlet on Turkey. This agitator – for he is one – undertook the task of proving his story by so called "genuine" testimony. With that aim in view, he published in his pamphlet some anonymous letters, about which, however, he wrote in an "explanatory note" the following: "It must be borne in mind that no writer was an eye witness of the actual massacre. . . . The letters are largely based on the testimony of refugees from that region, or of Kurds and soldiers which participated in the butchery, and who had no hesitation in speaking about the affair in public or private."

It follows, therefore, that the testimony given by Mr. Greene is a second-hand testimony, or, rather, solely an Armenian testimony, for only children could believe Mr. Greene's assertion that genuine Kurds and genuine Turkish soldiers gave to American missionaries the details that Armenian agitators and their friends were striving to obtain. As for Armenian testimony, in one of our previous letters we have already shown that, according to the opinion of the best friends of the Armenians, the latter cannot be believed "even on oath."

# Letter Five

A convincing proof that the Constantinople riots were premeditated and organized by the Armenian revolutionary committees is to be found in the fact that Armenian newspapers, published out of Turkey, announced a few weeks before the occurrence of said riots that they would take place at Constantinople. The Turkish authorities knew besides from other sources that such would be the case, and they were fully prepared to meet any emergency provocation and intimidation seem to be the plan of the Armenian revolutionists- provocation to the authorities and intimidation to their co-religionists. Bloodshed is the crowning result of their criminal efforts, supported, we are sorry to state, by English and American public opinion.

Admitting that Americans have no direct interest in European politics, the partiality shown by them toward the Armenian instigators of disorder has no excuse. The reason of such partiality must be because the Armenians are Christians. Still, this is certainly a bad reason; for, in spite of their Christianity, the Armenians are certainly an inferior and unreliable race, which was just as inferior and just as destitute of any sterling qualities or fame at an epoch when it had its own government in Asia. In the present day, Armenians are scattered about all over Asiatic Turkey, and they constitute in any Turkish province the minority of the population, which fact alone makes the use of the word "Armenia" simply preposterous. There may be an Armenia out of Turkey, but surely there is no Armenia in Turkey. There are Armenians there, and that is enough. A New York newspaper the enmity of which to the Turkish Government is not denied, wrote lately the following:

> "The statement has been made and repeated until it has become trite, without, however, having any apparent effect upon some people, that there is no country now existent which can fairly be termed Armenia. Historical Armenia included the southwestern Caucasus, a section of northwestern Persia, and that portion of eastern Turkey now included in the provinces of Diarbekir and Harpoot. The Caucasus section is still predominantly Armenian in population, but under rigid Russian rule. The Persian

Armenians are relatively few in number, and are found chiefly in the plains of Salmas and in the city of Khoi. In the Turkish provinces there are but four sections, of limited area, that would even ten years ago be fairly called Armenian- the plain of Moosh and Harpoot, the City of Van, and the Passen and Knus region, near Erzeroum. Already the Kurds, Circassians, and other Muslim tribes were driving them out, and within the past five years they have so nearly accomplished their purpose that today they probably far outnumber the Christians in those very sections. Where, then, are the Armenians? All over the empire."

To state, therefore, that there is an Armenia in Turkey is to make an erroneous statement. But erroneous statements on this Armenian question are so many that to contradict them all would be almost an impossibility. All these false statements originate from the Armenians themselves whose veracity is an unknown quantity. If Constantinople had been a small town in Asiatic Turkey, the Armenians would unmistakably have asserted, men as W. W Howard a the Rev. F.D. Greene, their assertions solely on Armenian testimony, would have promptly affirmed, that the Constantinople riots had as instigators not the Armenians, but the Turks, and that included, were tortured and killed by Turkish soldiers. Constantinople being where it is, even the Daily News, of London, that is to say, a newspaper whose policy is to try to ruin, if possible, and to destroy Turkey was obliged to remark:

"Two points ought, in justice to the Turks, to be noted. First, that it is beyond doubt that a large number of those Armenians who took part in the demonstration on Monday were armed. Secondly, the Government has not employed troops, nor allowed rifles to be used. The police were armed with revolvers, but the soldiers have only been employed as patrols, and I am not aware of any allegation of misconduct against them."

When, therefore, a European delegate, attached to the Commission of Inquiry that has been conducting an examination at the district of Sassoun into the alleged atrocities committed in that part of

Asiatic Turkey, says, as he does, that the allegations of Mr. Dillon and his Armenian friends are gross exaggerations, his statement must be true. Said delegate asserts most positively that the stories of wholesale massacre and violations of women, those connected with the number of killed which number fluctuates, strange to say, in one and the same pamphlet (we mean the slanderous pamphlet of the Rev. F.D. Greene) between 3,000 and 25,000 and those in relation to the finding of forty bodies buried in a pit at Gheliguzan, and to the throwing of Armenian women over a cliff to escape dishonor: all those ridiculous stories that made such a deep impression on credulous people already prepared to hate the Turk are, one and all, absolutely fictitious. The delegate moreover contends that the Armenians, instead of being remorselessly butchered while in a condition of helplessness, made a spirited stand against the troops, and were, just as during the Constantinople riot, armed. The European Commission of Inquiry has also proved that, instead of 30,000 Christians having been driven into exile, as alleged, the entire number of inhabitants of the disturbed district, Muslim and Christian, did not exceed 4,000.

However the administration of distant Turkish provinces may be, if even it were bad- and in that case it could be reformed the fact now remains that the so called Sassoun massacres have never existed. We do not say that no excesses have taken place there. In time of revolt, especially at places where the central government is powerless to exercise its influence, excesses do always take place. But the responsibility of those excesses lies with the criminal instigators of disorder, and that is precisely what the European and American public opinion, influenced by a huge religious agitation, refused to see and to admit.

One of the most prominent Armenians living in Constantinople, but who deprecates the foolishness of this Armenian agitation, gave the New York Sun, the following true version of the Sassoun revolt:

> "It was a regular battle, begun by our people attacking the Hamidié Kurdish troops (that is, committing an act of high treason), and perpetrating horrible cruelties on such Kurds as fell alive into their hands. These barbarous acts were the work rather of Armenian brigands, whom the revolutionists pressed into ranks, than of the villagers themselves, who by

no means are addicted to cruelty. Well, the fortune of war was favorable to the Armenians, who, partly armed with rifles, drove the Kurds before them, like a flock of sheep. They resolved to wipe out the Kurds once and for all, and would have done so if they had not been stopped in time: indeed, God only knows what would have happened. All Kurdistan would have been in revolt had it not been for the foresight and energy of Zekki Pasha, who ordered troops to march to the scene of the disturbance and soothe the ruffled spirits of the Muslims and Christians. Then, to be sure, certain excesses were committed, mainly by the Kurds, who were thirsting for revenge."

The increased agitation since Sassoun, on the part of the Armenian revolutionists in the Turkish provinces, and in Constantinople itself, proves in a forcible and clear manner time the above assertions are true to the letter. But, unfortunately, it is a very hard thing to convince people who are guided by secular prejudices or by political motives. Even Americans fail to perceive the political side of the Armenian intrigues in England. The Armenian agitation in the United States is not, it is true, political. It is merely religious, based not upon the intrinsic merits of the Armenians, which are totally lacking, but upon the fact that they are Christians. The result is that Armenian intrigues are upheld, both by English and American public opinion, although fatally tending to an armed rebellion in Turkey. The Missionary Boards are, we believe, to a great extent to blame for this disturbance of the sense of fairness on the part of Americans. The missionaries evidently trust time, by helping the Armenians in this emergency by organizing relief funds, and by having the money distributed to the Armenians alone, to the exclusion of any other nationality which latter fact is a very curious one, supposing that there is a general famine out there they would increase later on the field off their operations and usefulness, which means that they would make more converts to Protestantism, although the Armenians are already Christians. What would Europe and America say if the Turks were to exercise- which they do not- the doctrine of proselytism? Would they call it persecution?

# APPENDIX

The *Boston Advertiser* of May 21, 1895, published, about Admiral Kirkland's special report on Armenian affairs, the following telegram:

"Washington, May 20 - The Navy's investigation of the recent Armenian troubles throws doubt on the reports that atrocities were committed.

"The report of this investigation, which has just been received at the Navy Department, is made by Rear-Admiral Kirkland, Commander-in-Chief of the European Squadron. The ships of this squadron are now on their way to Gibraltar from the Mediterranean coast of Asia-Minor, where they have been cruising, attempting to substantiate the reports that the Sultan's soldiers outraged Armenians.

"The report is dated at Alexandriatta, the latter part of April, and states that all the ports the Marblehead and San Francisco, the vessels comprising the squadron, called at, they found American citizens working at their usual avocations, and apparently undisturbed by acts of molestation on the part of the Turkish Government. Their interrogation by the officers of the ships developed the fact that nothing had occurred to disturb them in their occupations, and that they had not been interfered with in any way.

"Admiral Kirkland states that rumors of atrocities in the Armenian country had reached the ports, but they lacked verification. Some of the most improbable stories of cruelties were told, but when they were traced to their origin it was found that there was nothing in them. He examined a number of people in the hope of obtaining some substantiation of 'cruelty' reports, but his examination invariably failed, and he gave it as his opinion that the reports had been very much exaggerated.

"The Admiral exonerates the Sultan from all blame in connection with the trouble between the Kurds and Armenians. 'The Sultan had as much to do with this trouble,' he says, 'as had the Governor of Massachusetts.'

"His conclusion that there were no atrocities is concurred in by the diplomatic representative of the United States with whom he came in contact during the cruise."

The *New York Herald* of August 18, 1895, published, about Admiral Kirkland's opinion on American missionaries in Turkey, the following telegram:

"London, August 17, 1895. - The United States cruiser San Francisco will on Tuesday next proceed to Havre, where she will go into dock to be cleaned and overhauled. The work will take at least a fortnight, and much longer unless the vessel is ordered away by the United States Navy Department.

"Rear-Admiral Kirkland, commanding the European station, whenever he speaks upon the subject, is emphatic in his condemnation of the missionaries in Turkey. He says that he has found that one of the most prominent Sunday-school teachers in Syria spent three years in the Penitentiary at Pittsburg, Pa., and that, taken altogether, they are a bad lot. The cause of all the trouble, Admiral Kirkland asserts, is that, relying upon the protection of the American Government, the missionaries defy the local laws, and do not merit the dispatch of a war-ship at every appeal made by the missionaries, most of which appeals are not true."

Extract from the *Boston Globe* of November 2, 1895:

Rev. Judson Smith, Secretary of the A.B.C.F.M., talked with a *Globe* reporter last evening, in regard to the reported attempt to burn the American college at Marsovan, Asia Minor. He said in substance:

"While I have no definite information in regard to the details of the reported incendiary attempt, I doubt if the Turks themselves are responsible. Strange as it may seem, we have more to fear continually from Armenians than we have from the Muslims.

"The reason for this fact is found in the inimical feeling aroused among members of the Armenian revolutionists society who have been expelled from the college at various times during several years past, because we cannot approve of their political course, and are consequently unwilling to be held in any way responsible for their unlawful measures or actions.

"American missionaries have always been loyal to the Turkish government and laws, and have avoided everything in any way calculated to indicate sympathy with Armenian revolutionary plots. Those revolutionaries are like the Russian nihilists, and cannot accomplish any good purpose. The Armenians, as a people, lack the cohesiveness and singleness of purpose necessary for success; they have not the political sense that made it possible for Bulgarians to become a nation.

"The whole aim of the Armenian revolutionists seems to be to keep up such a perpetual broil in the Turkish Empire that eventually Europe will feel compelled to break up the power of the Turk. Whether Armenians commit crimes, or are themselves the victims of Turkish outrages, is all the same to the revolutionists; whoever is the victim, their game is still played. This sort of thing is abetted by Armenians in America and elsewhere, and it is a great pity they could not all be kept in their native land. Members of this society will get into our college sometimes, and we feel obliged to expel them, hence incurring their enmity and threats.

"I am not surprised," continued Mr. Smith, "at the reported assassination of Mr. Garabed, who was understood to be a marked man by the revolutionists. He was a Protestant Armenian and one of the most prominent citizens in his community, as well as a good friend of the missionaries. It is quite likely he was murdered by Armenians; but I am sure it must be a mistake when it is reported that he was or had been one of the revolutionists and had been expelled from the college on that account. I am very sure that he was too old a man to have been a student there at any time since the college was started, in 1886.

"This is not the first attempt to burn the institution. Threats have been made against the principal officials of the college for years, and about five years a new building with it was burned. It was the girls' building, although I don't think that the fact had anything to do with its selection for destruction, but rather its situation, which gave better opportunity for the incendiary to escape without detection.

"We have already suspected the Armenian revolutionists of being guilty of that offence, but we never absolutely fixed it upon any individual. There was evidence, however, of the presence of Turkish police officials, under such circumstances as to render it almost certain that they were at least indifferent spectators of the affair, and, although very unwillingly, the Turkish Government was brought by the United States to so regard the matter that they ultimately gave us over $2,000 toward a new building."

Mr. Smith says the college has now about 180 young men students and 100 girls. Dr. C. C. Tracy, who has been in charge since its foundation, and Prof. Edward Riggs have been especially marked by members of the revolutionary party, and the Turkish Government some years ago granted them a guard for their better protection.

Mr. F. Hopkinson Smith, the artist and writer, told to a *New York Tribune* reporter the following about Armenians in Turkey:

"The turning point of the entire difficulty in this Armenian matter is this: No subject of Turkey can leave his country without first obtaining a government permit to do so. This is easy enough to secure if he can show that he has business interests calling him away, and armed with it he can go away and remain as long as he desires and ultimately return to his home. But those of Armenians are not doing this. In one way or another, they make their way out of Turkey clandestinely and at once come to the United States. Here they remain long enough to secure their declaration of citizenship. Then they secure passports as American citizens and at once return to their homes, with the sole purpose of acting as agents for one of the many revolutionary societies. If caught, which they are sure to be, they claim the protection of the American Minister, hoping thus to save their heads. It is in this that the United States are at fault. Under no other government can they carry out such a design. They cannot do it in England, or France, or Germany, or Russia - only in America.

"How they get out of Turkey I am not prepared to say, although there are numberless methods to be adopted. They can get down to Athens, or go by way of Sofia, or possibly they might be able to work their way up through Bulgaria. Anyway, the fact remains that they do elude the vigilance of the Government and with only one object in view. Why, just before I left Constantinople an Armenian was arrested, having a passport. He had in his possession forty-one revolutionary documents when arrested, and was armed besides. Yet Minister Terrell secured his release. This man in his trial before the Minister declared that he had come to this country simply to secure immunity from punishment by appeal, in case of arrest, to the American Minister, and that his purpose was to aid the revolutionists. I consider it a distinct outrage that this should be permitted.

"Another thing – There is not the slightest hope for the Armenians in case of an uprising. The Turks outnumber them in any part of the country three to one, and this reminds me of still another thing, which should be forcibly brought to the attention of the various missionary societies. They should be warned in time of the danger of sending missionaries over there, for in case of trouble they will assuredly be killed. Nothing can save them. An illustration of the hopelessness of the Armenian cause is to be found in the recent massacre at Stamboul. I was in Stamboul only two days before that massacre occurred. The Armenians had gone up ostensibly to present a peaceful petition to the Grand Vizier. Yet nearly every one of them was later on found to be heavily armed, and when the officers tried to disperse them, as being where they had no right to assemble, under Turkish law, they resisted, and the rest is known. The officials were clearly in the right.

"It is a saying in Constantinople that one Hebrew is good for two Greeks, a Turk is good for two Hebrews, and an Armenian can dispose of all of them. The Armenians are looked upon as the terrors of the community. They are the serving people of Turkey. The men act as porters, and I have seen two of them place an upright piano on their backs and wall straightaway up a hill of Péra. They are canny boys, I can tell you, and very muscular; but they are in a hopeless minority, and the Muslims hate them as they do the devil. I feel assured that England will one day regret the attitude she has taken on this question, but I am naturally more interested in the position of the United States. Judge Terrell, our minister here, is working day and night. He is indefatigable and upright and just. He has the respect of the Sultan, too, to a remarkable degree; but then America is held in high esteem by the Sublime Porte. I was sufficiently long in Constantinople to study these things with some degree of care. At first I did not pay much attention to them, for my profession is far apart from the consideration of such matters; but insensibly I was drawn into it, and I can safely assure the Tribune that I am telling only the bare facts as they exist."

The following contains Mr. F. Hopkinson Smith's opinion on Turks and American missionaries:

"I've just returned from Constantinople," said Mr. F. Hopkinson Smith, the author and artist, to a *Boston Herald* representative in New York two or three days ago. "While there I had an opportunity, through talks with Minister Terrell and two of the Sultan's aides, to learn all the inside facts about the Armenian atrocities. The whole matter has been grossly misunderstood, if not misrepresented, in this country. The root of the trouble lies in the missionaries sent out to Armenia from England and America. Instead of trying to help the people, they teach them that they are ill-treated, and sow the seeds of discontent and rebellion. They have started all the difficulty, and when the blame is properly placed it will rest upon their heads.

"We hear a great deal in this country about 'the barbarous Turk.' Now, I have traveled and painted all over the globe, and know pretty well the inhabitants of all countries; and let me tell you that I never met a more civilized, humane, intelligent, cleanly, pious, and chaste man than the typical Turk. He is quiet and respectable; he is preeminently kind and good to his family, and his religion enters into every part of his life. On my former visit to Constantinople, four years ago, I met a good many Muslims, and during my recent visit I came to know many more Turks of the best classes; and I make that statement without hesitation.

"For instance, I spent several days painting in the streets of Constantinople. The Sultan would not give a permit to do this, because he had refused such a privilege to divers Englishmen, and he did not wish to establish a dangerous precedent. He sent an official to accompany me on my trips, and every day that man left me three times and went into the mosque to say his prayers. Just think of the power of a religion which makes every man of a whole nation lay aside his business three times every day and prostrate himself toward Mecca in prayer!

"Go out here in Wall Street and try to persuade the people to go to church three times a day. You couldn't club them into it. The best of them only attend service once or twice a week. What are we, as a religious nation that we should attempt to force our religion upon every other nation on earth? We might as well start out to make silk hats for the world, and club every head into the right shape to fit them.

"See how humane the Turks are to animals. I don't know how many hundred thousand dogs there are in Constantinople, but probably there are fifty to the block. Every few minutes, if you are watching what goes on around you, you will see a Turk go over to the bake-shop, buy a bit of bread, or something else that dogs will eat, and feed them. Nobody owns these creatures. They have been common property for a thousand years, I suppose: yet, ugly and mangy as they are, they never go hungry. Nor do they ever suffer violence. Striking a dog in the streets of Constantinople means imprisonment for a year. Why, I've seen a team come along one of those narrow streets when a dog was lying in the way, and the driver would stop his donkeys and lift the dog out of the way, rather than run the risk of hurting him. I never saw any one beat or kick a donkey in Turkey. The people recognize that these creatures are their faithful servants, and treat them kindly. The love existing between the Turk or the Arabian and his horse is proverbial.

"What have we in the way of religion to teach these people? Nothing. It's pure bumptiousness for us to try to 'convert' them. They neither want nor need or religion. They've got a better one of their own. Better for them, I mean, not for us. They are already more religious, as a people, than we are.

"Another point. What order of men are they whom the English and the American religious bodies send out as missionaries? If you have ever noted closely the students in our training-schools for the ministry you must have discovered that as a class they are far from representing the best, or even a very good, type of American manhood. Many of them are young men from country towns and villages who could not make a decent living in any other calling. They go to these schools, in many instances, because they can get their education at half price, or free. Of course their poverty is no disgrace; but they are poor in every sense of the word. They hear a sermon by some returned missionary, who wishes to arose interest in the country in which he has lived, and straightway they are called to labor in the same field. Such sermons are apt to take hold of the less intelligent and more impressionable men, and it is often the men who are not fitted to take the high rank among the ministry in their own country who feel themselves drawn to work in a foreign land. The result is that we send out the most incapable specimens of our rural population - men of uncouth manners, who have learned a little Latin and Hebrew, the representatives of half a dozen religious sects, which are at constant war with each other about their creeds- to convert a cultured, courteous, pious, humane, temperate race, whose unified religion enters as much into the life of its members as does their business.

"Now and then we hear of some girl in a country town who thinks she has a mission to do good to the heathen. She had far better go down to the factory in her own village and minister there; but no, there is no glamour about that. Imagining that she is a new Joan of Arc, our hysterical friend tells some missionary body all about it, and they send her over to Turkey. You can picture to yourself the amazement and disgust with which the Turks regard such missionaries. Superb specimens of physique, they look upon these little wizened, dried-up, spectacled women with infinite contempt; just as they scoff at the idea of adopting a religion of which the various schools cannot agree.

"Well, colonies of such boors and cranks go over to Armenia, or somewhere else, and found schools. The children come to be taught, and eventually they join some one or another Christian church. They are pariahs as long as they live - marked boys and girls, branded men and women, who have lost caste among their fellows. What have they gained? 'Christianity,' you may say. Very true, but if they would lead pure and noble lives, under the religion of Muhammad, how are they better off? We surely cannot believe that heathen who lead good lives according to their lights do not go to heaven.

"Pretty soon some one comes along and hits an Armenian over the head. The missionaries keep telling their converts and the poor people that the Turk did it. They tell them they are abused, and stir them up to rebellion. The result is bloodshed, as you have seen. Here on my desk is a letter just received from Mr. Terrell, with whom I had many conversations in Constantinople. He says: 'We have certain information that 10,000 have been killed within a month.' That official statement, of course, includes those slain on both sides.

"He adds another statement, equally significant, to the effect that, so far as can be learned, not one American missionary has been injured. The Turks like the Americans who come to Constantinople far better than the Englishmen and they like America better than England, partly because as a nation we do not meddle with their affairs. When I have been painting in the streets I have never been subjected to discourtesies from the crowd which always assembled to watch me, except two or three times; and on those occasions the reason was that they supposed I was an Englishman. When they learned I was an American they ceased to annoy me, and even apologized for their rudeness. And they carry this esteem for Americans to the point of sparing our missionaries, even when the latter have sown the seeds of discontent in the hearts of their subjects."

Taken from the pamphlet, *Kurds and Armenians*, by S. Ximenez:

"Without wishing to extol the Kurds, although it seems to be the fashion now to charge them with all kinds of outrages, and to describe them as most savage hordes, I may state that I know them thoroughly, as I have seen them closely and lived with them for months. I met the first Kurdish tents one day's distance from Angora, and since then I never lost sight of them until I arrived in Lazistan. I saw, on my journey through Galatia, Cappadocia, Mesopotamia, and the districts which are situated in a northern direction towards the Black Sea, sometimes Turks, and at other times Armenians, Arabs, Chaldeans, Greeks, and Copts, but I never was one day without seeing Kurds. I was thus able to observe that the Kurds belonging to the great nomad tribes are harmless, whilst the Kurds settled in villages are sometimes to be blamed, and often to be pitied. In my opinion it is not absolutely necessary to look at humanity from an exclusively religious point of view. The idea of impugning systematically the Muslims in the of I do not know what principle, and merely because they are Muslims, strikes me as being quite out of place in this philosophical and tolerant century. In the present condition of the Asiatic provinces of the Ottoman Empire, nothing is more unfair and wicked than to try and create privileges for the sole benefit of one specific population. Such questions ought to be considered more liberally and from a higher standard. When I knew Anatolia only by what was published in European papers or said in the clubs at Péra, I must own that I shared some of the widely spread opinions, which appeared logical because brilliant and delusive. I had a somewhat vague notion of an Asia which must have been laid waste and given up to rapacious marauders; of periodically ransacked Christian villages, where any one who was not a Islamic could not possibly live; and I thought that I understood then the great crusades undertaken on behalf of the oppressed, the appalling stories circulated by itinerant preachers, and the emulation of so many people who seem so anxious to play the part of victims whereby they might secure a handsome income. Well, I do not pretend that on the Anatolian tableland every one is happy; it is about the same there as it is even in the most civilized countries, where the government is proceeding smoothly and where almost every day some new progress is recorded. Whatever the admirers of the Turkish Empire, who would let us believe that everything is as well as it can be beyond the Bosphorus, may say to the contrary, I am of opinion that there is a crisis in Asia Minor, that some modifications are necessary, some of which are gradually carried on, whilst some others are prospective. But a great fact, which appears in a vivid light to all who have traveled through Asia Minor, is that happiness as well as sorrows are the common lot of every people, whatever their race and creed may be. Any other estimate of the difficulty merely displaces the question without settling it. Every one knows that the Turks are not exterminators. All the different people under the Ottoman rule have been able to preserve their own traditional way of living, with their special features, manners, hopes, and creeds. After so many centuries they are still integral-more integral, no doubt, than they would be if they had been independent; but also with intestine quarrels, or with struggles against a foreign enemy belonging to the same religion. I will not quote names, but it would not be difficult to mention a certain people which, having been most corrupt and devoured by its own vice, owes its salvation and the flattering advantage of being able now to consider itself a nation, to the Ottoman conquest. And if the Turks did not exterminate the conquered nations at a time when no one would have asked them to account for massacres, what use is it now to ascribe tendencies to them which are in opposition to their own interest and character?

"I have traveled much, and I do not know of any country where greater toleration prevails than in Turkey. A collection of isolated facts which happened at more or less long intervals of time, and in regions more or less isolated from each other, may, when cleverly compiled under the form of a general report, help to the making up of a crushing Blue Book. Until now it never occurred to any one in Europe to select from any police record all the murders, rapes, and robberies committed in one town during a defined period, and to draw the conclusion therefrom that the said town is exclusively composed of brigands and murderers. Yet these are the proceedings employed in regard to the Turkish Empire when some busybodies want to interfere with Turkish affairs. Instead of sifting the question thoroughly and taking into account the social condition of the country, with a view of remedying by logical means some unavoidable evils under particular circumstances, the critics are busying themselves with such complications, to which they are careful to add gross exaggerations, coarse language, and serious charges, which, while redundant and fetching, fail however to bring about a solution, and are often the cause of conflicts. It has become an easy task, one which is well received by the public, to shriek in the name of humanity; such shrieks are always resounding, and if hollow they are noisy. They are more eagerly listened to by sympathetic crowds than logic and reason and impartial statements, which require a full knowledge of facts and a through mastery of the subject. It would be interesting to ascertain how many really searching and substantial papers have been published on the Armenian Question since it has been debated in the English press. Amongst various travelers who have lately been through Asia Minor, only one, Mr. Lynch, has written on the matter, and it is to be wished that any one approaching the subject should expatiate upon it with the same passionless and unbiased judgment as this distinguished writer, who contributed some remarkable articles to the Contemporary Review a few months ago on that question. Although I do not agree with all he says, I cannot help owning that Mr. Lynch did not waste his time during his travels to Erzeroum, Van, Moosh, and Bitlis, and that his conclusion is both instructive and commendable. Another writer, Mr. Richard Davey, who recently sojourned in Constantinople, studying all the texts in regard to the affairs in Asia Minor, has just written an article in the Fortnightly Review which in my opinion is far reaching, as he boldly exposes the part played by the British element in the Turco-Asiatic conflicts. The article in question is noteworthy for its fairness and impartiality. Great and influential English Reviews, however, with contributors boldly expounding their opinions, are less in touch with a certain portion of the public than some small Boston papers, for instance, which are replete with reports about the Turks cutting open the head of an Armenian, wherein they introduce poisonous and maddening flies, a kind of torture which causes the greatest indignation amongst those who are simple enough to believe such wild stories. And the detractors of the Porte are always sure to be successful slanderers when they vituperate the Kurds, whose very name seems to have become synonymous with savage cruelty."

Taken from the pamphlet, *A Few Facts about Turkey, Under the Sultan Abdul Hamid II*:

"It is a fact that faithful and law-abiding Armenians are not only protected, but also employed in very high official positions, one of them even being, at the present moment, a Minister of the Imperial Crown. The fact is, also, that the Armenians in Turkey, numbering a little over 900,000 (for they are no more), have their own schools, that their language and literature are preserved, that their nationality is respect, that their leading men are promoted in the scale of high honors and positions, while Christian Europe and America have no care for the Jews, and while Catholic Spain has not allowed a single Muslim family to remain on its European territory, and has centuries ago expelled them all. The reason for this colossal difference lies in the fact that Islamism is indeed a religion essentially and radically tolerant. If it were not, Turkey would not have had at the present moment a single Christian subject in any part of her vast dominions, and, for the benefit of the Turks, there would not exist now what is called the Eastern question. Turks suffer in our days from the tolerance that forms an intrinsic and essential part of our religion. Europe and America ought to be thankful to them. Instead of that, we see not a few eloquent Christian fanatics who countenance in Turkey what certainly they would not encourage in their own countries, namely, insubordination and revolt. Is this justice?

"The same spirit of injustice to Turkey is shown in regard to the policy of Turkey toward the Armenians naturalized in the United States on their return to the country of their birth, and many unfair accusations are made against the Sublime Porte for its insisting, in the absence of any naturalization treaty between Turkey and America, upon applying a law which is both wise and necessary, and which has been promulgated long before the Armenian troubles has begun. A short statement of facts as they really are, and not as disguised by Turkey's detractors, will, it is trusted, be deemed useful for the understanding of the case.

"The law concerning Ottoman naturalization is dated January 19, 1869, and is as follows:

"'ARTICLE 1 - Every person born of Ottoman father and mother, or only of an Ottoman father, is an Ottoman subject.

"'ARTICLE 2 - Every person born on Ottoman territory, of foreign parents, may, within three years after attaining majority, claim as of right the character of an Ottoman subject.

"'ARTICLE 3 - Every major foreigner who has resided during five consecutive years in the Ottoman Empire may obtain Ottoman nationality by applying, directly or through an intermediary, to the Minister of Foreign Affairs.

"'ARTICLE 4 - The Imperial Government may, by extraordinary act, confer Ottoman nationality on the foreigner who, without having fulfilled the conditions of the preceding article, should be deemed worthy of this exceptional favor.

"'ARTICLE 5 - The Ottoman subject who has acquired a foreign nationality with the authorization of the Imperial Government, is considered and treated as a foreign subject; if, on the contrary, he is naturalized as a foreigner, without the previous authorization of the Imperial Government, his naturalization shall be considered as null and of no effect, and he will continue to be considered and treated in all respects as an Ottoman subject.

"'No Ottoman subject can, in any case, naturalize himself as a foreigner, except after having obtained a certificate of authorization issued in virtue of an Imperial irade.

"'ARTICLE 6 - Nevertheless, the Imperial Government may declare loss of the character of an Ottoman subject against any Ottoman subject who shall have naturalized himself in a foreign country, or who shall have accepted military functions under a foreign government, without the authorization of his sovereign.

"'In this case the loss of the character of an Ottoman subject shall entail ipso facto the interdiction of the return to the Ottoman Empire of the person who shall have incurred it.

"'ARTICLE 7 - The Ottoman woman who has married a foreigner may, if she become a widow, recover her character of an Ottoman subject by making declaration to that end within three years following the decease of her husband. This provision is, however, only applicable to her person. Her property shall be subject to the laws and general regulations controlling the same.

"'ARTICLE 8 - The child, even when a minor, of an Ottoman subject who has naturalized himself as a foreigner, who has lost his nationality, does not follow the status of his father, and remains an Ottoman subject. The child, even when a minor, of a foreigner who has naturalized himself as an Ottoman, does not follow the status of his father, and remains a foreigner.

"'ARTICLE 9 - Every person inhabiting the Ottoman territory is reputed an Ottoman subject, and treated as such, until his character as a foreigner shall have been regularly proved.'

"Armenians and their friends in America have witnessed publicly that the law, a copy of which has just been given, is applicable solely to Armenians, and to Armenians nationalized in no other country but in the United States. The very perusal of the law shows these accusations to be meant to misguide public opinion. The law is for all former Turkish subjects, with no reference to their nationality and creed, who might have been naturalized either in the United States or in any other country in Europe. Armenians, however, have no wish to seek for a European naturalization. The reason is threefold: First, Europe knows well the Armenians, while America does not. Second, the endeavors made by American missionaries to convert the Armenians, and to give them a certain education, considered by Mr. Ximenez as inimical to the Turkish Government, prompt the latter to give their preference to the United States. Third, Armenians consider the American law on naturalization more advantageous to their secret plans and intentions, for American passports do not, for instance, contain the following clause, that is always to be found on English passports:

130

"'This passport is granted with the qualification that the bearer shall not, when within the limits of the foreign state of which he was deemed a subject previously to obtaining his certificate of naturalization, be deemed to be a British subject, unless he has ceased to be a subject of that state, in pursuance of the laws thereof, or in pursuance of a treaty to that effect.'

"If such a wise clause were put on all American passports, Armenians who wish now to become American citizens, in order to hide themselves behind the protection of the United States Government, would very promptly abandon American citizenship altogether, to the great relief of the State Department of Washington. The proof that Armenians almost never get naturalized in good faith, but, with perhaps no exceptions, in order to make use, if possible, of the United States Government against Turkey, is shown by the following extract of an official report of the present able United States Minister at Constantinople, Mr. Alexander Terrell, who, under date of September 29, 1893, writes:

"'The European emigrant in the United States generally naturalizes in good faith: the Asiatic very rarely does. I am in a position to know that it is the rule, rather than the exception, that the Armenian returns soon after he is naturalized, and goes back with the intention of remaining.'

"The statement was made above that American missionaries' side, on the whole, with Armenian revolutionaries against Turkey. This statement is based on the written declarations made lately by the American Board of Control for Foreign Missions, who, instead of advising the Armenians to be law-abiding subjects of the Sultan, and to preserve a dignified silence until the result of the investigation about the Sassoun troubles is made known, considered more to the point to affirm the existence of cold-blooded massacres, when that Board ought to have known that no cold-blooded massacres of any kind are countenanced by the Turkish Government, and that very presence in Turkey of American missionaries and

American schools, missionaries and schools existing principally for the conversion of Armenians to Protestantism, proved beyond doubt the tolerant spirit of the Turkish institutions. If American missionaries continue to side with discontented Armenians in Turkey, they will follow a policy contrary to the wish of the American Government and people. Turkey, at all events, must have peace at all costs in her territory, and she is justified in resenting the following admission made by an Armenian about the participation of Americans in the Bulgarian affairs of 1875:

"'I see of late,' writes that Armenian to the Boston Herald, 'Rev. Cyrus Hamlin has been writing letters of sympathy and support to the various meetings held in this country in behalf of the Armenians, in unmistakable terms as to his present attitude toward their cause. Several years ago I heard him lecture at Amherst, Mass. How proud he was to his audience the important part taken by the Bulgarian graduates of Robert College in securing the freedom and independence of their country! I ask Rev. Cyrus Hamlin if he was not aware of the existence of patriotic societies among his Bulgarian students, etc.'

"According to a French saying, we are betrayed by our friends. Let American missionaries and their Board realize that it is not their duty and mission to help in 'securing the freedom and independence' of any nationality in Turkey, or to countenance secret societies, or to accuse before the world the Turkish Government of massacres that have not and cannot have any existence in reality. Their duty is simple enough. It consists in confining their policy and utterances to the strict observance of the laws of the country that gives them hospitality. While, therefore, it is to be wondered why American missionaries, instead of devoting all their energies and good intentions on American Indians or on American negroes, choose to go to Turkey to educate in a certain fashion, and to convert, if possible, Christian Armenians to Protestantism; and while it is a fact that the Sublime Porte, thanks to the teachings of tolerance of its predominant religion, is willing to allow them, under its laws, to pursue their work; no one in all fairness could blame Turkey for manifesting uneasiness for the public utterances and written statements inimical to her government, made lately by the Board of said missionaries, and tending to encourage further revolt and further disturbances on her territory. The United States would certainly not allow such a guilty manifestation on the part of any foreign missionaries that might come here to educate and convert our Indians, for example, especially if the latter were implicated, as Armenians acknowledge themselves to be, in revolutionary schemes. What is right for the United States, why should it be right for Turkey? The Armenian agitation, based on falsehoods and exaggerations, and also on a pre-arranged plan, as described by Rev. Cyrus Hamlin himself, has been supported and intensified by many people for the only reason that the Armenians are Christians, which fact tends to prove that mere fanaticism animates Turkey's detractors. If this were not the case, the irresponsible and wild allegations of revolutionary Armenians would never have been believed and commented upon by people who call themselves impartial, without corresponding and convincing proofs. Turkey, therefore, sees now that she cannot implicitly rely on impartiality and on justice."

The following is a letter which will be read with interest as containing further evidence of the guilty interference on the part of American missionaries in Turkey. It was addressed to the *Boston Herald*, and signed by Mr. F. Hopkinson Smith, already quoted:

"In an interview with one of your reporters some days since, I made some statements regarding the condition of affairs in Turkey which came under my immediate notice. These remarks have created some astonishment and no little anger among many good people interested in the cause of foreign missions.

"The interview was, in the main, correct, certain allowances being made for a picturesque style of delivery more the reporter's than my own, and for certain conflicting statements in regard to the Sultan's being a humane man and at the same time giving permits to murder his subjects – the first of which is true and the last, of course, absurd. I am often astonished at the memory of the reporter, and slips like these are common to all interviews. I must disclaim, however, all reference to our missionaries as 'cranks and boors.' It has never been my habit to speak of a woman earning her bread in any department of life, missionary or otherwise, in any such terms, and I do not propose to begin now.

"As many of my statements have been charged to insufficient information on the condition of the Turk, dense ignorance of the past and present results of missionary work, mental bias, etc., I add to them the following data:

"In support of my statement that 'the missionaries sow the seeds of discontent and rebellion,' I quote from a distinguished Spanish traveler, Señor Ximenez, fellow of the Royal Geographical Society of England, who, on his return to London, immediately after the Sassoun troubles of a year ago – the first of these disturbances - was quoted as follows in an English journal:

"Señor Ximenez is disposed to lay much of the blame for the disturbed condition of Armenia on the American Methodist missions in Asia Minor. He says that they give the Armenians a superficial education out of all proportions to the need of the community. The pupils of these missions, he adds, are never satisfied to return to their homes and work their land. They continually speak of American liberty, and in nearly every case, says Señor Ximenez, the Armenian agitators are shown to have been pupils of the Methodist missions.'

"Second, as regards the helpless and law-abiding Armenian, I quote from a letter written by Rev. Cyrus Hamlin, published as far back as Dec. 23, 1893, in the *Congregationalist*, which, in view of recent events, is prophetic. Dr. Hamlin says:

"'An Armenian "revolutionary" party is causing great evil and suffering to the missionary work and to the whole Christian population of certain parts of the Turkish

Empire. It is a secret organization, and is managed with a skill in deceit which is known only in the East. In a widely distributed pamphlet the following announcement is made at the close:

"'This is the only Armenian party which is leading on the revolutionary movement in Armenia. Its center is Athens, and it has branches in every village and city in Armenia, also in the colonies. Nishan Garabedian, one of the founders of the party, is in America; and those desiring to get further information may communicate with him, addressing Nishan Garabedian, No. 15 Fountain Street, Worcester, Mass., or with the centre, M. Beniard, Poste Restante, Athens, Greece."

"'A very intelligent Armenian gentlemen,' continues Dr. Hamlin, who speaks fluently and correctly English as well as Armenian, and is an eloquent defender of the revolution, assures me that they have the strongest hope of preparing the way for Russia's entrance to Asia Minor to take possession. In answer to the question as to how, he replied: "These Huntchaguist bands, organized all over the empire, will watch their opportunities to kill Turks and Kurds, set fire to their villages, and then make their escape into the mountains. The enraged Muslims will then rise and fall upon the defenseless Armenians, and slaughter them with such barbarities that Russia will enter, in the name of humanity and Christian civilization, and take possession."

"'When I denounced the scheme as atrocious and infernal beyond anything ever known, he calmly replied: "It appears so to you, no doubt; but we Armenians are determined to be free. Europe listened to the Bulgarians horrors and made Bulgaria free. She will listen to our cry when it goes up in the shrieks and blood of millions of women and children." I urged in vain that this scheme will make the very name Armenian hateful among all civilized people. He replied:  "We are desperate; we shall do it."

"Third, as regards the superiority of the Islamic religion for the Islamic over any religion we can give him, I quote from Hon. Robert Curzon's *Armenia*, published by

Murray in 1854, pages 234-235. Curzon was the British member of the commission appointed by England, Russia, Turkey, and Persia in 1842, for fixing the then uncertain boundary between Turkey and Persia:

"'The superiority of the Islamic over the Christian cannot fail to strike the mind of an intelligent person who has lived among these races.... The Turk obeys the dictates of his religion, the Christian does not; the Turk does not drink, the Christian gets drunk; the Turk is honest, the Turkish peasant is a pattern of quiet, good-humored honesty, the Christian is a liar and a cheat; his religion is so overgrown with the rank weeds of superstition that it no longer serves to guide his mind in the right way. It would be a work of a great difficulty to distinguish the pure faith preached by the apostles from the mass of absurdities and strange notions with which Christianity is encumbered in the belief of the villages in out-of-the-way places, among the various sects of Christians in the dominions of the Sultan. This seems to have been the case for centuries, and it has produced its effect in lowering the standard of morality and injuring the general character of those nations who are subjects of Turkey and not of the Islamic religion. For, of the two evils, it is better to follow the doctrines of a false religion than to neglect the precepts of a true faith.'

"I also quote from an interview with a leading Armenian, published two weeks since in the *New York Tribune*:

"'If any people can know what real Christianity is, we are the people; and we are proud of our faith and of the heroism of our ancestors, who fought and died and were martyred for the cause of Christ. But the missionaries are not satisfied with our style of Christianity, and insist on converting us to their form of belief. Their work, while it has added so many thousand of names to their list of proselytes, has also brought discord to homes, has disrupted families, and has given rise to strife and controversy.'

"No one need lose his temper over this matter, and abuse is neither logical nor courteous. Much more additional data could be given, but the above is sufficient to convince reasonable people that there are two sides to the Armenian question."

# Bibliography

Al-Ahari, Muhammed Abdullah (2006), *Islam in America and Other Writings by Muhammad Alexander Russell Webb*, Chicago: Magribine Press.

Ali, Noble Drew (1927). *Holy Koran of the Moorish Science Temple.* Chicago: privately printed.

Boston Advertiser *(May 21, 1895). "Review of Admiral Kirkland's special report on Armenian Affairs."*

Boston Globe *(November 2, 1895). "Review of Admiral Kirkland's special report on Armenian Affairs."*

*The Critic*, January 25, 1896, No. 727, "*A Few Facts about Turkey under the Reign of Abdul Hamid II*," p. 61.

*Fibre & Fabric*, Vol.XXI, No. 53, May 11, 1895, "Turkish Railroads and Industries," p. 140.

Greene, Rev. Frederick Davis (1895). *Armenian Crisis in Turkey – The Massacre of 1894: Its Antecedents and Significance.* New York: G.P. Putnam's Sons.

Hamlin, Rev. Cyrus (December 23, 1893). *The Congregationalist*, "Letter to the Editor."

*How One Saves an Empire.* (Quoted by Webb in his *A Few Facts about Turkey under the Reign of Abdul Hamid II, but without bibliographic reference.*

*Journal of the Chamber of Commerce of Constantinople* (April 7, 1894). "Balance sheets for the Agricultural Bank during the financial year 1307."

Melton, J. Gordon, *Biographical Dictionary of American Cult and Sect Leaders* (Garland Publishing Company, Inc., New York & London, 1986), pp. 303 - 304.

*The Missionary Herald* by the American Board of Commissioners for Foreign Missions, Vol. XCI, No. 5, May 1895, "*A Few Facts about Turkey under the Reign of Abdul Hamid II*," pp. 177-178.

*New York Herald (August 18, 1895). "Review of Admiral Kirkland's special report on Armenian Affairs."*

*The Open Court*, Vol. X-30, No. 465, July 23, 1896. "The Armenian Troubles and Where the Responsibility Lies," p. 4998.

*Popular Science*, August 1895, Vol. XLVII - 35, "A Few Facts about Turkey under the Reign of Abdul Hamid," page 565.

Tunison, Emory H., "Muhammad Webb, First American Muslim," *The Arab World*, Vol. 1, No. 3, pp. 13-18.

Webb, Muhammad Alexander Russell (1896). *The Armenian Troubles and Where the Responsibility Lies*, New York: Press of J.J. Little & Co.

Webb, Muhammad Alexander Russell (1895). *A Few Facts about Turkey under the Reign of Abdul Hamid II*, Press of J.J. Little & Co.

Webb, Muhammad Alexander Russell (1893). *Islam in America, New York:* Oriental Publishing Company.

Webb, Muhammad Alexander Russell (1892). *The three lectures of Muhammad Alexander Russell Webb: delivered at Madras, Hyderabad (Deccan) and Bombay, with a brief sketch of his life,* Madras, India: Lawrence Asylum Press.

Ximenez, Santurnino. (1895). *Kurds and Armenians*, London.